Erdener Kaynak
Editor

Cross-National and Cross-Cultural Issues in Food Marketing

Cross-National and Cross-Cultural Issues in Food Marketing has been co-published simultaneously as *Journal of International Food & Agribusiness Marketing,* Volume 10, Number 4 1999.

Pre-publication
REVIEWS,
COMMENTARIES,
EVALUATIONS . . .

"**T**his book makes a significant contribution to our understanding of why food marketing and distribution systems differ among nations and cultures, and how to analyze, design and manage effective food marketing systems in an increasingly global economy."

Marius Leibold, PhD
Professor in Strategic Management
and Director of the Center
for Global Business
University of Stellenbusch, South Africa

D0073172

"**A**nd yet another classic book edited by Erdener Kaynak. Having lived and worked in three continents, I am absolutely delighted to see such a comprehensive book dealing with so many real issues in one of the most under-studied and under-researched fields of global marketing, global food marketing. Carefully selected articles highlight quite cleverly the unique aspects of global food marketing, cover a wide range of processed and unprocessed food products and provide authoritative opinions pertaining to food marketing in Africa, Asia, Europe and North and South America. The book is destined to be an essential reading for managers, public policy makers, researchers, students and teachers of food marketing in developed, developing and underdeveloped countries."

Muammer Ozer, PhD
*Assistant Professor of Marketing
and Management
City University of Hong Kong*

"**T**his is an excellent and timely book in the food marketing over the purely social/economic framework has been broadened to include different country environments. Whilst the Canadian, North American and European problems in food marketing have been addressed, additional insights into areas such as Pakistan and Spain have enriched conventional ranking. A strength of this special issue is that a variety of conceptual frameworks, models and marketing procedures allows generative thinking into some of the issues and problems facing food (and especially meat) marketers."

Alma Whiteley, PhD
*Professor and Acting Director
Graduate School of Business
Curtin University
Perth, Australia*

"**E**dited by one of the most distinguished authorities in international marketing. Or Erdener Kaynak, *Cross-National and Cross-Cultural Issues in Food Marketing* is a meticulously researched book that well help both food marketers and public policy decision-makers better understand the issues that affect food marketing and distribution in counties of different levels of development A complete understanding of world food marketing systems is only possible when they are examined from an economic development perspective rather than only from the perspective of the multinational corporation. In this sense, the book combines topics related to cross-national differences in food marketing and distribution, offering insights into marketing systems in different food categories and their respective distribution venues and mechanics. The models address various country-specific developments in specific areas of the food industry, such as the linkage between agricultural exports and economic growth in the Pakistan market, the ethnic niche markets for fresh Canadian pork in the united States Pacific Northwest, U.S. poultry exports, quality policy and consumer behavior with regard to beef in Spain,

and yogurt market segmentation in the European Union. This material is theoretically linked by a brilliant, insightful introduction by the book editor linking the different perspectives into a unified theoretical framework of food marketing and distribution.

This book is likely to benefit both marketing practitioners in the food industry and public policy decision-makers involved in the efficient delivery of food products to the population. It will benefit academics in the process of researching world food marketing and distribution issues, as well as academics teaching food marketing applications to their international marketing classes."

Dana-Nicoleta Lascu, PhD
Associate Professor of Marketing
University of Richmond, VA

"**F**ood marketing combines two crucial topics: *food*: which is the basis for life and survival, and *marketing*: which is the means by which we plan and develop products, pricing, promotion, and distribution. But the horizons are even wider now, as food marketing has the crucial role of feeding our world's teeming population. Because of the vast differences in eating habits between the peoples of our world, cross-national and cross-cultural issues in food marketing are brought to the forefront.

This expanded role for food marketing is truly exciting. Within our grasp is the ability to feed the world, in spite of vast differences in tasty, tradition, climate, the environment, and economics. Food marketers, knowingly or unknowingly have an increasing role, and responsibility, for ensuring that all people have access to tasty, safe, affordable, and nutritious food. What a marvelous challenge!

This book examines the role and importance of cross-national and cross-cultural issues in food marketing. But rather than delve solely in the past, the authors present us with powerful tools and finding which show us directions for the future. Within this book are discussions of the linkage between agricultural exports and economic growth, the impact of ethnic niche markets on imports, the increased importance of quality policies and consumer behavior, comparative advantage and competitiveness, and cross-cultural cogmentation.

This book brings us to Belgium, Brazil, Canada, China, Denmark, Greece, Japan, Saudi Arabia, Spain, Thailand, The United Kingdom, and the United States, among others. There will be discussions of beef, pork, poultry, yoghurt, and many other food products.

Many readers will find this book particularly useful, including food marketers, government policy makers, classroom teachers, and anyone with an interest in international business."

Michael F. Duffy, PhD
College of Business Administration
Minot State University
Minot, ND

IBP

International Business Press
An Imprint of The Haworth Press, Inc.

Cross-National and Cross-Cultural Issues in Food Marketing

Cross-National and Cross-Cultural Issues in Food Marketing has been co-published simultaneously as *Journal of International Food & Agribusiness Marketing,* Volume 10, Number 4 1999.

The *Journal of International Food & Agribusiness Marketing* Monographic "Separates"

Below is a list of "separates," which in serials librarianship means a special issue simultaneously published as a special journal issue or double-issue *and* as a "separate" hardbound monograph. (This is a format which we also call a "DocuSerial.")

"Separates" are published because specialized libraries or professionals may wish to purchase a specific thematic issue by itself in a format which can be separately cataloged and shelved, as opposed to purchasing the journal on an on-going basis. Faculty members may also more easily consider a "separate" for classroom adoption.

"Separates" are carefully classified separately with the major book jobbers so that the journal tie-in can be noted on new book order slips to avoid duplicate purchasing.

You may wish to visit Haworth's website at . . .

http://www.haworthpressinc.com

. . . to search our online catalog for complete tables of contents of these separates and related publications.

You may also call 1-800-HAWORTH (outside US/Canada: 607-722-5857), or Fax: 1-800-895-0582 (outside US/Canada: 607-771-0012), or e-mail at:

getinfo@haworthpressinc.com

Cross-National and Cross-Cultural Issues in Food Marketing, edited by Erdener Kaynak, PhD, DSc (Vol. 10, No. 4, 1999). *"A meticulously researched book that will help both food marketers and public-policy decison makers better understanding the issues that affect food marketing and distribution in countries of different levels of development."* (Dana Nicoleta-Lascu, PhD, Associate Professor of Marketing, Department of Marketing, E. C. Robins School of Business, University of Richmond, Richmond, Virginia)

Food and Agribusiness Marketing in Europe, edited by Matthew Meulenberg, PhD (Vol. 5, No. 3/4, 1994). *"Presents a wealth of information and material for conceptual and comparative analysis . . . Represents the state of the art in the study of food and agribusiness in the EU."* (The European Review of Agricultural Economics)

Cross-National and Cross-Cultural Issues in Food Marketing

Erdener Kaynak, PhD, DSc
Editor

Cross-National and Cross-Cultural Issues in Food Marketing has been co-published simultaneously as *Journal of International Food & Agribusiness Marketing,* Volume 10, Number 4 1999.

International Business Press
An Imprint of The Haworth Press, Inc.
New York • London • Oxford

Published by

International Business Press®, 10 Alice Street, Binghamton, NY 13904-1580

International Business Press® is an imprint of The Haworth Press, Inc., 10 Alice Street, Binghamton, NY 13904-1580 USA.

Cross-National and Cross-Cultural Issues in Food Marketing has been co-published simultaneously as *Journal of International Food & Agribusiness Marketing* ™, Volume 10, Number 4 1999.

Cover design by Thomas J. Mayshock Jr.

Library of Congress Cataloging-in-Publication Data

Cross-national and cross-cultural issues in food marketing/Erdener Kaynak, editor.
    p. cm.
    "Cross-national and cross cultural issues in food marketing has been co-published simultaneously as Journal of international food & agribusiness marketing, volume 10, number 4, 1999."
    Includes bibliographical references and index.
    ISBN 0-7890-0963-3 (alk. paper)–ISBN 0-7890-0981-1 (alk. paper)
    1. Food–Marketing–Cross-cultural studies. 2. Farm produce–Marketing–Cross-cultural studies. 3. Export marketing–Cross-cultural studies. I. Kaynak, Erdener.

HD9000.5 .C735 2000
380.1'456413–dc21   99-087756

INDEXING & ABSTRACTING

Contributions to this publication are selectively indexed or abstracted in print, electronic, online, or CD-ROM version(s) of the reference tools and information services listed below. This list is current as of the copyright date of this publication. See the end of this section for additional notes.

- *Abstracts on Rural Development in the Tropics (RURAL)*

- *AGRICOLA Database*

- *BIOBUSINESS: covers business literature related to the life sciences; covers both business & life science periodicals in such areas as pharmacology, health care, biotechnology, foods & beverages, etc.*

- *Biosciences Information Service of Biological Abstracts (BIOSIS)*

- *BUBL Information Services: An Internet-based Information Service for the UK higher education community <URL:http://bubl.ac.uk>*

- *Business & Management Practices*

- *Cabell's Directory of Publishing Opportunities in Business & Economics (comprehensive & descriptive bibliographic listing with editorial criteria and publication production data for selected business & economics journals)*

- *CNPIEC Reference Guide: Chinese National Directory of Foreign Periodicals*

- *Food and Nutrition Information Center*

- *Food Institute Report "Abstracts Section"*

- *Food Intelligence on Compact Disc (covers the food industry, including journals in business, foodservice management, aquaculture, biochemistry, food preparation, irradiation, microbiology, nutrition and toxicology)*

- *Food Market Abstracts*

- *Food Science and Technology Abstracts (FSTA), Scanned, abstracted and indexed by the International Food Information Service (IFIS) for inclusion in Food Science and Technology Abstracts (FSTA)*

(continued)

- *Foods Adlibra*

- *IBZ International Bibliography of Periodical Literature*

- *Referativnyi Zhurnal (Abstracts Journal of the All-Russian Institute of Scientific and Technical Information)*

- *Violence and Abuse Abstracts: A Review of Current Literature on Interpersonal Violence (VAA)*

- *World Agricultural Economics & Rural Sociology Abstracts, c/o CAB International/CAB ACCESS . . . available in print, diskettes updated weekly, and on INTERNET. Providing full bibliographic listings, author affiliation, augmented keyword searching*

Special Bibliographic Notes related to special journal issues (separates) and indexing/abstracting

- indexing/abstracting services in this list will also cover material in any "separate" that is co-published simultaneously with Haworth's special thematic journal issue or DocuSerial. Indexing/abstracting usually covers material at the article/chapter level.
- monographic co-editions are intended for either non-subscribers or libraries which intend to purchase a second copy for their circulating collections.
- monographic co-editions are reported to all jobbers/wholesalers/approval plans. The source journal is listed as the "series" to assist the prevention of duplicate purchasing in the same manner utilized for books-in-series.
- to facilitate user/access services all indexing/abstracting services are encouraged to utilize the co-indexing entry note indicated at the bottom of the first page of each article/chapter/contribution.
- this is intended to assist a library user of any reference tool (whether print, electronic, online, or CD-ROM) to locate the monographic version if the library has purchased this version but not a subscription to the source journal.
- individual articles/chapters in any Haworth publication are also available through the Haworth Document Delivery Service (HDDS).

Cross-National and Cross-Cultural Issues in Food Marketing

CONTENTS

ABOUT THE EDITOR

Erdener Kaynak, PhD, is presently a Professor of Marketing and Chair of Marketing Program at the School of Business Administration of The Pennsylvania State University at Harrisburg. During 1985-1986 academic year, he was a Visiting Professor of Marketing and International Business at The Chinese University of Hong Kong. For the first half of 1992-1993 academic year, he served as a Visiting Professor of International Marketing at Helsinki School of Economics and Business Administration in Helsinki, Finland and for the second half, he was a Visiting Professor of Marketing at Norwegian School of Management, Oslo, Norway. He also served as Visiting Professor of Marketing at Bilkent University in Ankara, Turkey during the summers of 1989 and 1991 as well as serving as Visiting Professor of Marketing at University of Hawaii at Manoa; Curtin University of Technology, Perth, Australia; Odense University and The University of Aalborg, Denmark; Fukuoka University, Japan; City University of Hong Kong, Hong Kong; University of Macau, Macau; Bishkek International School of Business and Management, Kyrgyz Republic.

Dr. Kaynak holds a B.Econ (Hons.) degree from The University of Istanbul, an M.A. in Marketing from the University of Lancaster, a Ph.D. in Marketing Management from Cranfield University (formerly The Cranfield Institute of Technology) and an honorary D.Sc degree in Business Administration from Turku School of Economics and Business Administration in Finland. So far, he has taught at Hacettepe University in Ankara, Turkey, Acadia University in Wolfville and Mount Saint Vincent University, Halifax, Nova Scotia, Canada. He also served as Chairman of the Department of Business Administration at Mount Saint Vincent University for a period of six years and Assistant Director for Research and Planning at the School of Business Administration of The Pennsylvania State University at Harrisburg for two years. Furthermore, he has conducted post-doctoral research studies at Michigan State University, East Lansing, Michigan, U.S.A.; The Universities of Lund and Uppsala, Sweden; The University of Stirling, Scotland; The University of Stellenbosch, Stellenbosch, South Africa; and The Helsinki School of Economics and Business Administration, Helsinki, Finland.

Dr. Kaynak has lectured widely in diverse areas of marketing and international business and has held executive training programs and trained business persons and government officials in five continents at over thirty countries of Europe, North and Latin America, Africa, The Middle East, The Far East including The People's Republic of China and Australia. He is the founder and

President of a Halifax, Nova Scotia based company, Cross-Cultural Marketing Services Incorporated. His professional expertise lies in such areas as international marketing, export marketing, marketing in developing countries, services marketing, food marketing and distribution, comparative marketing systems, tourism marketing, bank marketing, strategic marketing planning, small business exporting, tourism and hospitality marketing planning, business education development, privatization of state enterprises, islamic banking, marketing and economic development, business case development and writing, and project management.

Cross-National and Cross-Cultural Issues in Food Marketing: Past, Present and Future

Erdener Kaynak

SUMMARY. The present economic crisis and cost efficiency consider-ations in countries around the world at varying levels of economic devel-opment makes marketing and distribution related decisions and policies both at micro (individual company level) and at macro (sector or country level) of paramount importance. In studying the food marketing systems around the world, one has to take environmental differences in these coun-tries into consideration. That is the reason why marketing institutions and processes are structured to respond to the most important environmental dimensions of the countries. The purpose of this article is to evaluate the current state and likely developments of food marketing and distribution systems. As well, constructs and conceptual frameworks were also devel-oped for the study of food marketing and distribution practices. An at-tempt is made to use a typology of economic systems for less-developed countries to illustrate how current food marketing and distribution systems are affected by the current economic systems of the countries at a different level of development. *[Article copies available for a fee from The Haworth Docu-ment Delivery Service: 1-800-342-9678. E-mail address: getinfo@haworthpressinc. com <Website: http://www.haworthpressinc.com>]*

KEYWORDS. Cross-national and cross-cultural food marketing, envi-ronment of food marketing systems, different countries/regions, eco-nomic systems, government control, levels of planning

---

Erdener Kaynak is Professor of Marketing and Chair of the Marketing Program, School of Business Administration, Pennsylvania State University at Harrisburg, Middletown, PA 17057 USA

[Haworth co-indexing entry note]: "Cross-National and Cross-Cultural Issues in Food Marketing: Past, Present and Future." Kaynak, Erdener. Co-published simultaneously in *Journal of International Food & Agribusiness Marketing* (International Business Press, an imprint of The Haworth Press, Inc.) Vol. 10, No. 4, 1999, pp. 1-11; and: *Cross-National and Cross-Cultural Issues in Food Marketing* (ed: Erdener Kaynak) International Business Press, an imprint of The Haworth Press, Inc., 1999, pp. 1-11. Single or multiple copies of this article are available for a fee from The Haworth Document Delivery Service [1-800-342-9678, 9:00 a.m. - 5:00 p.m. (EST). E-mail address: getinfo@haworthpressinc.com].

INTRODUCTION

Food marketing systems evolve within the confines of socio-economic, cultural, legal-political and technological environments of countries. To understand and explain the basis and rationale behind a given country's food marketing system, one has to look at the components (institutions, processes as well as functions performed by actors of the system) and their evolution into their present state. The distinction between food marketing systems in developed countries and those in developing economies cannot be based solely on the presence or absence of certain marketing institutions and organizations. Generally, all forms of marketing institutions will be found virtually in all marketing systems. Thus, it will not be useful to attempt to classify economies by stage of food marketing system development on the basis of the availability or unavailability of particular structural elements, unless their relative importance–both volume, productivity and effectiveness–can also be delineated.

The present economic crisis and cost efficiency considerations in individual countries as well as across nations at varying levels of socio-economic development, make food marketing related decisions and policies both at micro (individual firm level) and macro (societal or country level) of paramount importance. In order to be more effective in global consumer markets and be more sensitive to different food marketing strategy decision areas, North American and West European companies are becoming more and more interested in the marketing systems and processes of other countries. To this end, we are witnessing the development of a "consumer-driven" food marketing system. This, in most cases, includes changes in demographics and diverse life-styles, diet and health considerations that change eating patterns, concerns for food safety, innovative marketing and retailing practices, and agricultural production impacts (Senauer et al. 1993).

The purpose of this volume on cross-national and cross-cultural issues in food marketing is to evaluate the present state, and likely developments of food marketing systems in different country environments. An attempt is also made to develop constructs and conceptual frameworks for studying food marketing systems across countries and/or cultures. Some working propositions have been formulated in an effort to establish a sound base for studies in the field of comparative food marketing systems. It must be pointed out here that most of the studies, so far, have been descriptive and exploratory in nature. What is needed is theory formation and testing of the existing constructs and propositions in a number of developing country environments for the purpose of deriving generalizations.

LEVEL OF DEVELOPMENT

In a study of food marketing system development, the first step may be to evaluate the level of market development in countries at a different level of development. So far, only a few studies have emphasized the importance of determining the degree of economic development (Kaynak 1986). A number of authors have dwelled upon measuring the degree of market development which would enable the researcher to classify countries accordingly (Litvak and Banting 1969; Hansz and Goodnow 1972). Unless the countries are grouped together on the basis of their economic development, it will be difficult to study the food marketing systems and practices in the countries of one group and determine the finer nuances in their marketing practices so that they could be compared with the next group. The development of systematic and sound approaches to determine the degree of socio-economic development in the countries of the world is still very much needed.

The food marketing system's relative economic importance to the rest of the economy has been declining as consumers all around the world have been spending a declining share of their income on food purchases (Gallo 1991). Food manufacturing and marketing firms domestically as well as internationally have introduced more new and varied products to satisfy ever smaller targeted consumer markets. For instance, the U.S. food sector is blending more and more into the global food market. In most cases, overseas markets offer U.S. food companies tremendous opportunities for expanded sales. Many U.S. food companies frequently enter international markets through the use of licensing or franchising agreements with firms overseas. Although exports are traditionally thought of as the primary way of access into overseas markets, manufacturing foods abroad is the major way large U.S. food processors reach international markets (Anonymous 1996).

ENVIRONMENT OF FOOD MARKETING SYSTEMS

An environment refers to what is external to a food marketing system and neither directly controls it nor is directly controlled by it. Marketing scholars have interpreted the prevalent marketing practices in terms of socio-economic conditions of a country. One cannot deny or undermine the effects of socio-economic factors, but one must also consider that other environmental factors, for example, the supplier environment, competition and legal and governmental legislation and actions, may also affect the characteristics of food marketing system of a country.

The proposition that the marketing system of a country is closely related to the development of its social, economic and cultural environments is widely accepted. However, the precise nature of the relationship between environmental factors and the marketing system is a matter of speculation (Douglas and Craig 1992). A food marketing system seeks to satisfy human needs, but the manner in which it performs its functions varies among different countries. It can purposefully by hypothesized that a pattern of food marketing systems, in terms of the type of institutions, retailing practices, organization of firms, managerial attitudes and channel structure, may be expected to emerge within countries under the influence of various environmental conditions. The interaction taking place between the distribution system and the surrounding environment is shown in Figure 1.

The new food marketing system in a country is subject to several limitations: the number of potential customers, their incomes, and their social and

FIGURE 1. Interaction Distribution Systems and the Marketing Environment

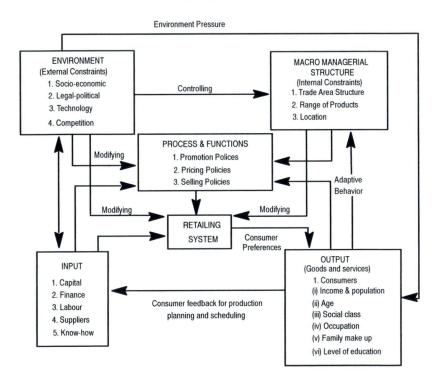

Source: Adapted from Erdener Kaynak, "A Refined Approach to the Wheel of Retailing," *European Journal of Marketing*, Vol. 13, No. 7, p. 242

economic make-up. Each sets a different limit on the number of units demanded for the new institution. Likewise, available managerial talent, financial resources, initiative and capital place different limits on the number of units that could be operated profitably. The growth of the new food marketing system is, to a certain extent, contingent upon easing the restrictive input limitation.

At present, there is change and development going on in the food marketing systems of countries around the world whether developed or developing. The causes of these are environmental, and these are, to a large extent, beyond the control of the existing food marketing system. For that reason, environmental conditions should be taken into consideration while designing an ideal food marketing system for a country.

FOOD MARKETING AND ECONOMIC DEVELOPMENT

The role of food marketing in developing countries is changing as economic development takes place. Three different situations, which reflect stages of economic development, may be distinguished: Situation I is characterized by the predominance of many small scale traditional distributors and is typical of the least developed countries, as experienced in many cities of Tropical Africa. Situation II relates to cities with well established specialized grocery stores and limited-line stores, a structure such as existed in Central and Northern Europe forty years ago, which is now common in many urban centers of Latin America, in some lesser developed Mediterranean countries and in the more highly developed Near and Far Eastern cities. In these economies, specialized distributors with a higher level of operation than that which prevails under situation I are needed. Situation III is applicable to those cities with higher consumer incomes, e.g., parts of Latin America and Western Europe, where integrated and associated food chains have developed. In this situation, the antecedent form of distributors perform only a supplementary function in supplying only a minor portion of the total market. Much of the essence of these changes of distributive forms may be synthesized in the role of economic development of a developing economy. With this process came the shift from production orientation to sales and at a later stage to consumer orientation. It also brought about improvements in distribution technology and managerial expertise. All of these forces interacted and stimulated each other. The result is that one can show changes in the distribution system along a continuum of economic development (Campbell 1974).

For illustrative purposes economic systems of developing countries at varying levels of development are described. This is done with reference to who owns the production facilities and what mechanism allocates resources (see Figure 2). A more realistic and useful conception of the alternatives is shown in Figure 3. In this figure, the whole range of alternatives between two extremes is shown on a scale of one to seven. At one end is a system where all business and economic decisions about prices, investment, distribution and marketing are made and planned by the government which may or may not be democratic (The Canadian Manufacturers' Association 1980).

Having determined the type of economic system prevalent in a developing country and key variables in organizing its economic systems, the next step would be making decisions on production and marketing issues. Some of the basic questions needing answers are listed as follows:

FIGURE 2. Key Variables in Organizing Economic Systems in LDCs

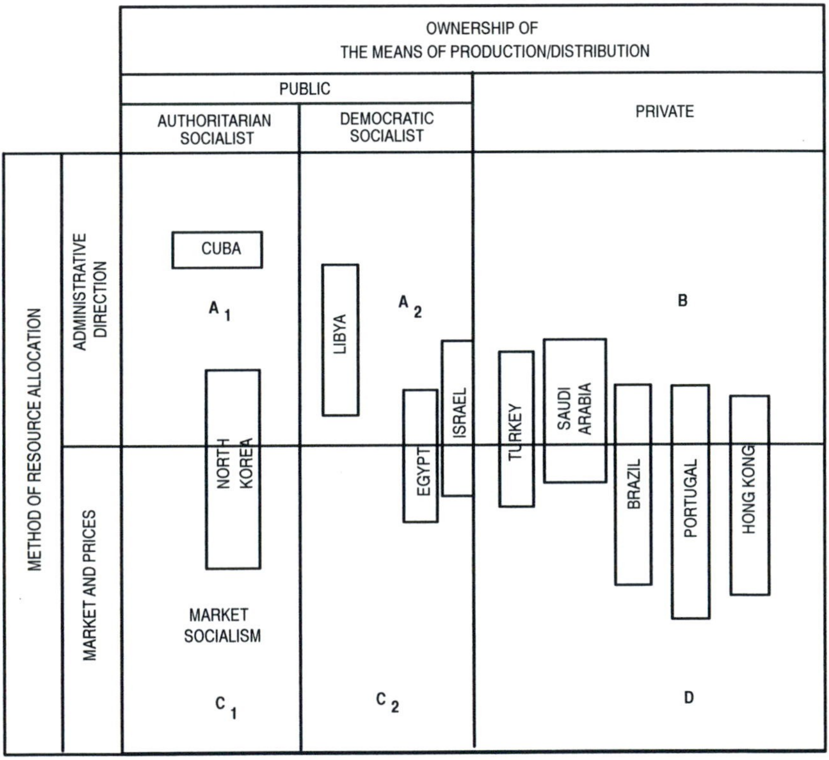

Source: Adapted from *Trade-offs: Some crucial economic choices*, Canadian Manufacturers' Association, Toronto, February 1980, p. 6.

FIGURE 3. Alternative Economic Systems for LDCs

HIGH←			DEGREE OF GOVERNMENT CONTROL				→ LOW
SCALE →	1	2	3	4	5	6	7
TYPE OF SYSTEM →	GOVERNMENT PLANNED CUBA		INDICATIVE PLANNING INDIA	MIXED ECONOMY TURKEY			COMPETIT MARKET MECHANISM HONG KONG
KEY INDICATORS 1. INDIVIDUAL FREEDOM	LOW			MEDIUM			HIGH
2. DISTRIBUTIVE SYSTEM	STATE CONTROL			PUBLIC-PRIVATE SECTOR COOPERATION			LAIZSSEZ FAIRE
3. RESPONSIVENESS TO CONSUMER PREFERENCES	LOW			MEDIUM			HIGH
4. TYPE OF GOVERNMENT POLICIES	POLITICAL & BUREAUCRATIC DISCRETION			BALANCED			NEUTRAL UNIVERSAL APPLICATION

Source: Adapted from *Trade-offs: Some crucial economic choices*, Canadian Manufacturers' Association, Toronto, February 1980, p.5.

1. What shall be produced according to whose preference?
2. How is it going to be produced and by whom?
3. Do we consume now, or save and invest for the future?
4. How will the output be distributed? (The Canadian Manufacturers' Association 1980, p. 7)

It is the last question that more time will be spent on here by exploring further. First of all, there are a multitude of factors involved in the development of a distribution system in developing countries. Among these factors are: (1) distributive functions performed, (2) distributive institutions utilized in the channel, (3) marketing management skills of the channel intermediaries, (4) cultural constraints, (5) socio-economic factors, (6) behavioral patterns, (7) legal-political and governmental factors, and (8) technological factors.

Past literature of marketing on developing countries indicate that distribution systems of these countries are backward and they do not match up with the improved production/manufacturing systems of these countries. However, there is ample opportunity for improvement in the distribution systems of these countries. This may take three different forms (Kaynak et al. 1999). The first is related to improvements in the physical appearance of market places, the second to improvements in distribution and marketing facilities and the third to the establishment of marketing extension services by government agencies.

CROSS-NATIONAL ISSUES IN FOOD MARKETING

Food marketing and distribution systems do vary among countries of the world depending upon their varying levels of economic and technological development. The primary purpose of the study by Henneberry and Khan is to examine the role of agricultural exports on the economic development of Pakistan. Understanding the impact of agricultural exports on Gross Domestic Product growth is important for effective public policy decisions and the timing of this information is critical as Pakistani policy makers now face major economic reforms in their quest for development. In this study, Pakistan is used as a case study due to its large amounts of agricultural exports, which have competed with industry for government support. The model used in this study is composed of a system of three simultaneous equations determining exports, imports, and GDP. The first equation specifies per capita agricultural exports as a function of real GDP, net factor income remittances from abroad, and investment. The second equation specifies per capita total imports as a function of the same exogenous variables as in the export equation. The third equation specifies per capita GDP as a function of agricultural exports, manufactured exports, total imports, net factor income remittances from abroad, and investment. This study utilizes time series data from 1971 through 1990. The results of this study indicate that a favorable relationship exists between agricultural exports and economic growth and that the agricultural sector should not be neglected in the process of industrial development. More specifically, this study shows that the amount of agricultural exports from Pakistan is positively related to Pakistani economic growth. The results of this study are consistent with the results obtained by others that have shown that the growth of the industrial sector is highly related to growth in the agricultural sector.

The ethnic Asian market in the states of Washington and Oregon constitutes a sizable niche market for fresh Canadian pork. The objectives of the study by Peter Kuperis et al. are to evaluate the Asian ethnic markets for fresh pork in the United States Pacific Northwest and Vancouver. Asian retailers and distributors in Vancouver, Seattle and Portland were surveyed by direct interview during November and December 1996. The survey applied semantic differential scaling questions, open-ended questions and a stated preference task, a conjoint methodology, to examine pork retailer's and distributor's perceptions of fresh pork produced in Western Canada and in the Midwest United States.

The structure of the market for fresh pork represented by retailers catering to Asian consumers in Vancouver differs from that in Seattle and Portland. The "Asian market" in Vancouver is dominated by many small shops that deal directly with packers. The small shops in Seattle and Portland deal with distributors and wholesalers. Distributors play a small role in Vancouver's retail market. Asian retailers in Seattle deal with a variety of suppliers, including both packers and distributors. In Portland, retailers catering to Asian consumers trade mainly with distributors and a local packer-wholesaler.

The survey results show Western Canadian pork enjoys an image of superior quality amongst retailers and distributors in Seattle's ethnic Asian market. Asian retailers in Portland are less familiar with Western Canadian pork and did not regard it as highly as did retailers in Seattle. Distributors in Portland are more familiar with Western Canadian pork and consider it to be superior to Midwest United States pork in terms of overall quality, meat color and fat trim. In both markets, Western Canadian pork is generally considered to be expensive. These results are not statistically significant; however, they are of economic relevance since most of the major players in the segment were interviewed.

Western Canadian pork presently enjoys a reputation for superior quality amongst the retailers that specialize in sales to Asian consumers in Seattle and Portland. However it is also clear that many members of the trade lack information or experience with Canadian pork. There is an opportunity for Canadian processors to maintain or increase market share through more education and promotion to this market segment.

The article by J. Briz et al. focuses on quality policy and consumer behavior with regard to fresh meat. Challenges for the meat demand sector have been of great concern due to a decrease on consumption in many European countries. Therefore a research project (FAIR-CT 95-0046) was developed on this field.

The negative trend in beef, veal and pork demand made necessary the implementation of quality programs, which differentiates between hygiene and safety, health and quality. In the area of safety there are mandatory minimum standards. In hygiene there is an application of the HACCP method in some enterprises.

In order to restore consumers' confidence in fresh meat, some several quality actions are followed, such as traceability from producer to retailer and labeling. All the quality programs in the Spanish meat sector have been initiated by farmers or meat industries and their associations. A number of special private institutions have been created for assessing each scheme. Besides that, some public organizations are directly engaged in the regulation, implementation and promotion of quality programs.

According to the consumer survey, the more important characteristics in beef and veal are flavor, tenderness, and juiciness. Color and smell are in second position. The main concerns are hormones content in beef and salmonella in chicken.

Several efforts should be undertaken to get back consumer confidence. Public policy should separate between regulating quality and safety. Promotion programs should involve traditional retailers and consumer associations. Traceability and regulation should be performed by private enterprises and public institutions.

The general objective of the study by Kristin Michel et al. is to analyze the comparative advantage and future prospects of the U.S. poultry industry in the international arena. The domestic resource cost (DRC) ratio was estimated for the five largest poultry exporters in the world. The DRC ratio provides a comparison of economic advantages/disadvantages in poultry trade. In addition, an analysis of the future of international poultry trade was conducted based on published forecasts.

Published studies have shown that poultry production and consumption are expected to increase in most countries. The United States, having one of the better DRC ratios, is predicted to retain its majority position in international poultry trade as export growth slows in the European Union and Thailand. However, domestic production in Hong Kong/China will pose a threat to U.S. exports along with the expected growth in the Brazilian poultry industry.

The future of international poultry trade is likely to change in several ways. The strong demand for high priced white meat in the U.S. domestic market is supporting the low cost of dark meat and other poultry pans exported to foreign market, particularly in Southeast Asia. The expected growth in the Brazilian poultry industry can also affect international trade considering that the Brazilian domestic market prefers dark meat over white meat. Finally, the continued economic problems in Russia and Southeast Asia will dampen future U.S. poultry export growth.

The paper by Carlotta Valli et al. discusses the strategic importance of developing research on international segmentation of food markets, particularly in the light of increased internationalization of competition. An increasingly competitive international environment makes it necessary for firms to focus more and more on cross-country consumer segments.

The objective of the paper is to present an application of market segmentation to the European yogurt market aimed at identifying cross-country consumer segments sharing similar characteristics and product preferences. The segmentation of the yogurt market is based on a relatively innovative consumer measure, means-end chains. The means-end chain approach links consumer preference for product attributes with benefits sought from product consumption and with values, considered by much consumer research literature to represent consumers' ultimate motivation to product choice.

The results of the segmentation exercise show that the means-end segments identified hold interesting implications for the development of marketing strategies at a pan-European level. The results suggest that, for their very nature, means-end segments provide particularly useful information for the development of new product ideas, concepts for product positioning and market communication, which can be standardized to some extent. Besides the strategic implications of such cross-country segments for the development of appropriate marketing programs, more general managerial implications are pointed out. First of all, the identification of pan-European consumer groups sharing similar needs allows for the expansion of target markets across borders. At the same time, the standardization of marketing programs should lower marketing costs and make it possible to exploit economies of scale in both production and marketing communication. A closer identification of consumer needs is also expected to translate into better information for European consumers and improved choices through the development of better targeted marketing strategies and better differentiated products. However, market competition and the structure of the yogurt manufacturing and retailing sectors in the various countries will continue to determine the degree to which marketing programs can be standardized, particularly with respect to pricing and distribution strategies.

REFERENCES

Anonymous (1996), "Setting Course for Global Food Markets," *Food Review*, Washington; Vol. 19, May-August, pp. 2-4.

Campbell, R.W. (1974), "Stages of Shopping Center Development in Major Latin American Metropolitan Markets," *Land Economics*, Vol. 50, No.1, (February), pp. 66-70.

Canadian Manufacturers' Association (1980), *Trade-Offs: Some Crucial Economic Choices*, February, Toronto, Canada.

Douglas, Susan and Samuel Craig (1995), *Global Marketing Strategy*, McGraw Hill, Inc, New York, pp. 312-333.

Gallo, Anthony E (1991), "The Food Marketing System at a Glance," *Food Review*, (July-September), pp. 38-43.

Hansz, J.E. and J.D. Goodnow (1972), "A Multivariate Classification of Overseas Country Market Environments," in B.W. Becker and H. Becker (eds.) *Combined Proceedings*, American Marketing Association, Chicago, pp. 191-198.

Kaynak, Erdener (1986), *World Food Marketing Systems*, Butterworth Scientific Publishers, London, pp. 3-13.

Kaynak, Erdener (1986), *Marketing and Economic Development*, Praeger Publishers Inc, New York.

Kaynak, Erdener (1987), "Cross-Cultural Food Buying Behavior," *Food Marketing*, Vol. 3, No. 3, pp. 34-49.

Kaynak, Erdener, Ali Kara, and Berrin Guner-Dosoglu (1999), "Channels of Distribution in Developing Countries: Past and Emerging Trends," in *Proceedings of the 8th World Business Congress of The International Management Development Association*, Monterey, CA.

Litvak, I.A. and P.M. Banting (1969), "A Conceptual Framework for International Business Arrangements," in R.L. King (ed.) *Marketing and the New Science of Planning*, American Marketing Association, Chicago, pp. 460-467.

Senauer, Ben, Elaine Asp, and Jean Kinsey (eds.)(1993), *Food Trends and the Changing Consumer*, University of Wisconsin Press, WI.

An Analysis of the Linkage Between Agricultural Exports and Economic Growth in Pakistan

Shida Rastegari Henneberry
Muhammed E. Khan

SUMMARY. This article examines the relationship between agricultural exports and economic growth. Pakistan is used as a case study due to its large amounts of agricultural exports which have competed with industry for government support. This study estimates three simultaneous equations representing GDP, agricultural exports, and total imports while incorporating factors such as income remittances from abroad, investment, and manufactured exports as independent variables. The timing of this information is critical as Pakistan's policy makers now face major agricultural reforms in their quest for development. The estimation results show that a favorable relationship exists between agricultural exports and growth in GDP. *[Article copies available for a fee from The Haworth Document Delivery Service: 1-800-342-9678. E-mail address: getinfo@haworthpressinc.com <Website: http://www.haworthpressinc.com>]*

KEYWORDS. Agricultural exports, economic growth, Pakistan, agricultural reforms

Shida Rastegari Henneberry is Professor of Agricultural Marketing Policy, Department of Agricultural Economics, Oklahoma State University. Muhammed E. Khan is affiliated with Oklahoma State University.

Constructive input of Becky Nelson, graduate research assistant, is gratefully acknowledged.

The research for this paper was partially funded through Hatch project No. H-2242 of the Oklahoma State University Agricultural Experiment Station.

[Haworth co-indexing entry note]: "An Analysis of the Linkage Between Agricultural Exports and Economic Growth in Pakistan." Henneberry, Shida Rastegari, and Muhammed E. Khan. Co-published simultaneously in *Journal of International Food & Agribusiness Marketing* (International Business Press, an imprint of The Haworth Press, Inc.) Vol. 10, No. 4, 1999, pp. 13-29; and: *Cross-National and Cross-Cultural Issues in Food Marketing* (ed: Erdener Kaynak) International Business Press, an imprint of The Haworth Press, Inc., 1999, pp. 13-29. Single or multiple copies of this article are available for a fee from The Haworth Document Delivery Service [1-800-342-9678, 9:00 a.m. - 5:00 p.m. (EST). E-mail address: getinfo@haworthpressinc.com].

INTRODUCTION

More than one billion people in the world today, the majority of whom are located in developing nations, live beneath international poverty standards among conditions of intense deprivation (Tisch and Wallace, 1994; Ty, 1994). Despite national and international efforts to change this situation, and despite decades of aggressive lending policies on the part of foreign aid programs, many developing nations throughout Latin America, Africa, Asia, and the Middle East are worse off today than they were 20 years ago (Bandow and Vasquez, 1994). While the true measure of these nations' development needs to be expressed through improvements in quality of life, their economic growth plays a significant part in this process by both providing increased per capita income and increased available revenue for government sponsored social services.

One particular sector which has been given special attention in development strategies is agriculture. Agricultural products, particularly those with export potential, have been viewed by many underdeveloped nations around the globe as playing a vital role in economic development. Senegal's "New Agriculture Policy" lists peanut exportation as one of its goals in its attempt to achieve sustainable economic growth (Ndaiye, 1994). Ghana's economic reform policies have strongly promoted timber exports and also supported cocoa production for export (Hommond and McGowen, 1994). Costa Rica has shifted state support from traditionally produced products for domestic markets to the production of high value non-traditional agriculture exports in hopes of stabilizing its economy and to bring in much needed foreign exchange (Korten, 1994). Given the emphasis on agricultural exports by some countries as the path to economic development, a study of the effect of agricultural exports on a nation's development would be useful to policy makers in understanding the impacts of economic policies. A study focused on an individual nation is necessary in order to account for all the factors that are truly unique to a nation's economy.

The overall objective of this study is to determine the effect of Pakistan's agricultural exports on economic growth. Pakistan is used in this research as a case study. Like many of today's other developing nations, Pakistan's government is currently pushing for open-market reforms, and many of the programs and policies which have supported the agricultural sector may have been left by the wayside. With pressure being exerted for the removal of the agricultural subsidies and with the imminent restructuring of Pakistani economic policy, a study of the impact of Pakistan's agricultural exports on the status of its economy is timely.

In the first part of this study, an overview of domestic and international agricultural policies and structure is given. Next, the model and data used to analyze the impact of agricultural exports on economic growth are defined. Estimation results and conclusions are included in the final part of the study.

Agriculture and Agricultural Policies in Pakistan

Pakistan, a semi-industrial developing nation, was chosen as the focus for this study. From the beginning of independence, the agricultural sector has played a very important role in Pakistan's economic development. Nevertheless, the economy has gone through a gradual transition in which it shifted from mostly agricultural to the one with dominant agricultural and manufacturing sectors. During the fiscal year 1959-60, the agricultural sector accounted for 46 percent of gross domestic product, employed 59 percent of the labor force, contributed to 44 percent of total foreign exchange earnings, and accounted for 44 percent of exports (Table I). Thirty years later, during the fiscal year 1990-91, the agricultural sector's contribution to gross domestic product (GDP) declined to less than one fourth while agricultural employment remained over one half of the country's labor force. In 1990-91, the agricultural share of total foreign exchange earnings[1] declined to about one sixth, and the contribution of the agricultural sector to total value of exports declined to slightly more than one fourth (Table I). According to the most recent data (Finance Division, 1993), agriculture contributed to 24 percent and 47 percent of Pakistan's GDP and labor force employment during 1992-93. The declining contribution of agriculture to GDP relative to labor force employment may be an indication of the declining labor productivity in agriculture relative to other economic sectors.

Wheat, cotton, and rice are the main crops in Pakistan. Wheat is the main staple of Pakistan and is produced mainly for domestic consumption. Its share in total cropped area is around 40 percent. It is grown both in irrigated and unirrigated areas of all the provinces of the country. Pakistan achieved self-sufficiency in the mid-eighties; but during the years with heavy floods or other natural disasters, the country resorts to imports to meet the demand. Wheat production increased by 153 percent during 1970/71 through 1992/93 (Table II).

TABLE I. Agricultural Sector's Share of Labor Force, Gross Domestic Product, Exports, and Foreign Exchange Earnings, Pakistan, Selected Years.

Year	Share of Ag. In:		Share of Ag. Exports in:	
	GDP	Labor Force	Foreign Exchange Earnings	Total Value of Exports
	(percent)		(percent)	
1959-60	45.83	59.30	44.38	44.38
1971-72	36.02	57.32	39.53	39.53
1979-80	29.57	52.67	18.30	33.12
1990-91	25.70	51.50	16.69	28.89

(Source: Finance Division, Economic Survey 1991-92)

TABLE II. Cropped Area and Production of Wheat, Rice and Cotton, Pakistan, 1970-92.

Year	Wheat		Cotton		Rice	
	Area (000 hect)	Production (000 tons)	Area (000 hect)	Production (000 tons)	Area (000 hect)	Production (000 tons)
1970-71	5,977	6,476	1,733	542	1,503	2,200
1975-76	6,111	8,691	1,852	514	1,710	2,618
1980-81	6,984	11,475	2,108	715	1,933	3,123
1985-86	7,403	13,923	2,364	1,208	1,863	2,919
1990-91	7,911	14,565	2,662	1,637	2,113	3,261
1992-93	8,225	16,394	2,806	1,586	1,934	3,083

(Source: Finance Division, Economic Survey 1992-93)

Rice is another staple and is produced for not only the domestic market, but also for exports. In the world market, Pakistan has been among the top exporters of rice during the last decade. Pakistan is said to have a monopoly in the exports of basmati, which is high-valued aromatic rice (Dorosh and Valdes, 1990). In 1991, exports of rice accounted for six percent of total value of exports (Table III). Rice production increased by 40 percent during the 1970/71–92/93 period (Table II). Pakistan has also a significant share of the world cotton exports and cotton is considered to be the most important cash crop of Pakistan. Over the last decade, Pakistan has been among the top five exporters of raw cotton. Increased cotton production in Pakistan has allowed Pakistan not only to develop one of the largest textile sectors in the world, but also has been a significant source of income developed from exports. According to the most recent available data, raw cotton and cotton products have provided the country with almost 60 percent of its exports (Table III). Cotton production in Pakistan almost tripled from 1970/71 through 1992/93 (Table II).

Fish and fruits and vegetables are also exported from Pakistan (Table III). Nevertheless, Pakistan's exports of fruits and vegetables have been marginal. The absence of processing, grading, and marketing facilities as well as poor quality may have contributed to this poor performance (Ministry of Food and Agriculture, March 1988). Other agricultural and natural resource based products important to Pakistan's export sector include leather and leather manufactures, carpets and carpeting, and petroleum products; which accounted for 8.5, 3.5, and 1.2 percent of the value of exports during the fiscal year 1991-92 (Table III).

However, despite the importance of agriculture in Pakistan's economy, trade policy in Pakistan has had a clear bias toward promoting manufactured goods in external markets through export subsidies and protecting them in the domestic market through import restrictions such as tariffs, quotas, and bans. On the other hand, at times exports of some agricultural goods such as cotton

TABLE III. Percentage Share of Major Product Categories in Total Value of Exports, 1991-92.

	1991-92
Total Cotton group	58.2
Rice	6.0
Leather	3.8
Leather Manufactures	4.7
Fish and Fish Preparations	1.7
Carpets and Carpeting	3.5
Petroleum Products	1.2
Synthetic Textiles	6.3
Fruits and Vegetables	0.7
Others	13.9
Total	100.0

(Source: Finance Division, Economic Survey 1991-92)

and rice have been explicitly taxed or exports of other crops such as wheat have been banned. In the past, the government of Pakistan has viewed increased taxation of the large agricultural sector as a source of revenue to relax its budgetary problems. A related study shows that because Pakistan's major agricultural products such as wheat, basmati and ordinary rice, cotton, and sugar were consistently taxed, production of these crops suffered. It is estimated that during the 1983-87 period, without government price intervention, farm incomes from these major crops would have been 40 percent higher (Dorosh and Valdes, 1990).

Nevertheless, Pakistani agriculturists have been recipients of fertilizer, electrical, irrigation, and farm credit subsidy programs for many years (Dorosh and Valdes, 1990). In 1989-90 alone, these subsidies exceeded five billion Rupees (Nasim and Akhlaque, 1992). However, during 1978-87, the implicit tax on agriculture was about nine times the actual net subsidies to producers. Dorosh and Valdes estimate the net effect of price and non-price related income transfers for the five major crops (wheat, basmati and ordinary rice, cotton, and sugar) to be a transfer out of agriculture of approximately 25 percent of agricultural GDP during the 1978-87. To intensify matters, a strong voice is making itself heard in the call for explicit taxation of agricultural incomes, which currently constitutes only 4% of total tax revenues (despite the fact that agriculture accounts for 26 percent of GDP) and has historically been constitutionally exempt from such taxation (Nasim and Akhlaque, 1992). As Pakistan's government moves toward its new-found capitalistic goals, the protected agricultural policies may be viewed as inequitable which give the agricultural sector an unfair advantage over other allocations of resources.

International Trade Structures and Strategies

During the decade of 1982/83 through 1991/92, Pakistan's exports grew from $2.7 billion to $6.9 billion at current prices, a 156 percent increase (at constant prices, exports were $0.8 billion to $1.5 billion in 1982 and 1991, respectively). During this ten-year period, exports at current prices grew on an average of 11.3 percent per year. The growth of exports at constant prices was 7.5 percent per year during the same period. Moreover, Pakistan's exports have shown a positive change in their composition towards higher value products. From 1971/72 to 1992/93, the share of primary goods in total export value decreased from 45 percent to 15.9 percent, the share of semi-manufactured goods fell from 27 percent to 19.8 percent, while the share of manufactured goods rose from 28 percent to 64.3 percent. Increased export earnings from cotton manufactures and other non-traditional exports have contributed positively to export revenues. However, Pakistan's export sector is still concentrated in a few products including cotton and cotton manufactures (total cotton group) and rice, which together accounted for 64 percent of the total value of exports (Table III). This narrow export base and the lack of export diversification have made the country vulnerable to external shocks. Between 1980 and 1989, available data indicate that the concentration and diversification indices changed only marginally from 0.239 and 0.777, respectively in 1980 to 0.232 and 0.846 in 1989 (Finance Division, 1993).

During the two decades from 1971/72 through 1992/93, the import structure did not change as much as the export structure, but nevertheless the country has been increasing its imports of raw materials for consumer goods. During 1971/72, 23 percent of the imports were consumer goods, 24 percent were the raw materials to manufacture the consumer goods, 42 percent were capital goods, and 11 percent were the raw materials to manufacture the capital goods. In comparison, during 1992/93, 15.6 percent of imports were consumer goods, 39.0 percent were the raw materials to manufacture consumer goods, 40.1 percent were capital goods, and 5.3 percent were raw materials to manufacture the capital goods. From 1982/83 through 1991/92, imports grew from $5.4 billion in current prices to $9.3 billion, a 72 percent increase. In constant prices, imports grew from $1.6 billion in 1982/83 to $2.0 in 1991/92, a 25 percent increase. The average annual rate of import growth during this period was 5.5% per year at current prices and 2 percent per year at constant prices.

Regarding the competitive advantage of export products, a government study (Ministry of Food, 1988) of the analysis of agricultural export competitiveness indicate that Pakistan would be well advised to focus on its traditional crops, mainly cotton and rice (basmati in particular). The study also advises that the focus on cotton processing for exports should be primarily on yarn where no quantitative restrictions govern exports. The determination of

Pakistan's comparative advantage is based on the domestic resource cost estimates[2] which indicate that Pakistan in a global environment is an efficient producer of wheat, basmati and IRRI[3] rice, cotton, sugar cane, and fruits and vegetables (Ministry of Food, 1988).

PREVIOUS RESEARCH

Researchers have shown empirical evidence indicating the existence of a statistically significant and strong correlation between the growth rates of output and exports. It has been shown that the export sector results in positive externalities for the rest of the economy by better resource allocation, capacity utilization or reduced X-inefficiency, and by the introduction of technological breakthroughs to other sectors (Balassa, 1978; Tyler, 1981).

Another hypothesis suggests, contrary to neo-classical theory, that marginal productivities across different sectors in developing economies are not the same and that marginal productivities are expected to be higher in the exporting sector due to their exposure to competitive factors from abroad. However, it is argued that despite the higher marginal productivities present in the export sector (as compared to the domestic sector), resources are diverted away from the export sector. It is suggested that developing countries can grow not only with the expansion of factors of production, namely capital stock and labor force, but also by the reallocation of resources from the less productive non-export sector to the more efficient export sector (Feder, 1983).

Jung and Marshall have listed three factors which could be responsible for the positive correlation between real export growth and growth in real GNP. These factors are as follows: export growth directly contributes to growth in real GNP; increased exports lead to increased foreign exchange availability which may enable the economy to increase imports of intermediate and capital goods that in turn lead to growth in GNP; and growth in the export sector might result in positive externalities such as increased efficiency in the non-export sector, and these externalities would lead to growth in the GNP (Jung and Marshall, 1985).

Most previous research has concentrated on this last relationship. At present most developing countries are dependent on exports for foreign exchange. Although some of them have access to much needed foreign exchange in the form of foreign aid and private loans, exports are still the primary supplier. According to the theory of "two gap," the foreign exchange function of exports is only important when the economy is facing an import shortage resulting from a foreign exchange constraint. Most of the previous works have implicitly assumed that import shortage was not a problem with the countries included in their studies.

Esfahani carried out a study aimed at testing whether semi-industrialized countries (SIC) are indeed facing import shortage due to a binding foreign exchange constraint. Findings by Esfahani implied "that the positive impact of the exports on GDP observed in the past is likely to be due to the import-shortage reduction rather than the externality effect" (Esfahani, 1991).

MODEL AND DATA

The purpose of this study is to determine the relationship between agricultural exports and economic growth in Pakistan. The three stage least squares systems (3SLS) approach was used to estimate the equations in this study to avoid simultaneity bias. The selected model for this study has a system of three simultaneous equations determining GDP, exports, and imports. The equations also check for the possibility of import shortages due to binding availability of foreign exchange through the inclusion of income remittances from abroad in the imports equation. This has not been addressed in much of the existing literature. Each equation was also estimated using the ordinary least squares method (OLS), which evaluates each equation separately. While this method is highly susceptible to simultaneity bias, OLS can be a very effective tool for small samples since it minimizes the variance and is less susceptible to estimation errors including misspecifications.

The model used in this study assumes that economic growth is simultaneously determined along with agricultural exports and total imports. As proposed by Davidson and McKinnon, the J-test was used in the process of model selection, and only statistically significant variables were included in each of the three equations. This assures that the model is specifically tailored to the Pakistani economy (Davidson and McKinnon, 1981). A double-log (Cobb-Douglas) specification, which assumes constant elasticities, is used. The preliminary plots of economic, export, and import growths supported the choice of this functional form for this study.

Agricultural Exports Equation

The use of the J-test to narrow down the factors that determine the agricultural exports resulted in the exclusion of agricultural labor force from the model. This is due to the fact that its coefficient does not prove to be statistically significant (J-test). This may be attributable to the fact that Pakistani agriculture has been considered a labor surplus sector, so an increase in agricultural labor force might not result in a significant change in the size of agricultural exports.

One of the underlying assumptions behind the model used in this study is that Pakistan is a small country in the world market and its exports do not have any significant impact on world market prices. The following agricultural export function (Equation 1) was selected for this study:

(1) $\log(X_a)_t = \alpha_0 + \alpha_{GDP} \log(GDP)^t + \alpha_{NFI} \log(NFI)_t + \alpha_{INV} \log(INV)_t +$ Error

The real value of per capita agricultural exports is represented in this equation by the variable X_a. The per capita real (GDP) is expected to have a positive relationship with agricultural exports due to both economic theory and the externality hypothesis. Per capita net factor income remittances from abroad (NFI) was included in the equation due to its special significance in the Pakistani economy. NFI is defined as the funds that are earned by Pakistani citizens in foreign countries and were sent to Pakistan in foreign currencies.[4] As a significant factor in the Pakistani economy, it is important to determine the effect of income remittances on Pakistan's economic development. Per capita real investment (INV) is also included due to its potential for increasing productivity and efficiency, both of which are expected to change the amount of surplus of agricultural products available for exports.[5]

Imports Equation

By considering special features of the Pakistani economy, the following function (Equation 2) was used to represent Pakistani imports:

(2) $\log M_t = \beta_0 + \beta_{GDP} \log(GDP)_t + \beta_{NFI} \log(NFI)_t + \beta_{INV} \log(INV)_t +$ Error

All variables are as previously defined. Due to data limitations, total per capita imports (M), which include both consumer and industrial goods, were utilized in the equation rather than agricultural imports. Per capita GDP represents buying power which is in turn expected to affect the demand for imported goods.

GDP Equation

The GDP function is a modified form of the one used by Esfahani. The following function (Equation 3) was selected for GDP:

(3) $\log GDP_t = \gamma_0 + \gamma_{Xa} \log(X_a)_t + \gamma_{Xm} \log(Xm)_t + \gamma_M \log(M)_t +$ $\gamma_{NFI0} \log(NFI)_t + \gamma_{INV} \log(INV) +$ Error

In this equation, log is natural logarithm of the variable, t represents time, γs represent the parameters to be estimated, γ_0 is the intercept. The agricultural export variable was intended to provide data regarding both the relationship between GDP growth and agricultural exports, and also to help determine the validity of the externality hypothesis as applied to the agricultural sector. The share of manufactured goods in total exports (X_m) was used to assist in determining the impact of a change in total export structure on GDP growth. Comparison of the potential externalities created by agricultural exports with those created by manufactured exports is possible when manufactured exports are accounted for through this variable. All other variables are as previously defined.

ESTIMATION RESULTS

The equations for agricultural exports, imports, and GDP growth were estimated by several models. The Shazam (White et al., 1993) computer program was used for estimation. Each model utilized data from 1970 through 1990, and all results are reported in Table IV. The first model estimated all three equations, as originally defined, simultaneously using the three stage least squares method. The results from this complete model (Model 1) are reported in the first column of Table IV. In an alternative model (Model 2; Table IV, Column 2), the manufactured share of exports was excluded to examine the impact on the coefficient of the agricultural exports variable. In another modification of the model, the variable representing per capita imports and the import equation were dropped from the complete model. The results from this version are reported in the third column (see Model 3, Table IV). The fourth and the final model (Model 4, Table IV, last column) estimates each equation separately using the OLS single equation approach. The system R^2s for all three models reported in Table IV are high (0.98, 0.99, and 0.97 for models 1, 2, and 3, respectively), indicating that most of the variability in the dependent variables are explained by the independent variables. The R^2s for the three equations estimated using OLS (Model 4) are 0.57, 0.82, and 0.88 for the agricultural exports, imports, and GDP equations, respectively (Table IV). Moreover, the R^2s for each equation when all three equations are estimated as a system[6] are consistent with the single equation R^2s from the OLS method of estimation.

The relationship between agricultural exports and GDP growth was demonstrated by the estimated parameter (γ_{Xa}) for the independent agricultural export variable in the GDP equation and by the estimated parameter (α_{GDP}) for GDP growth in the agricultural exports equation. In all four models which estimated the GDP equation (Equation 3), γ_{Xa} was found to be positive and statistically significant at a level of one percent. According to these models, a one percent increase in per capita agricultural exports would ultimately result in an increase of 0.22 to 0.36 percent in per capita GDP. This result supports

TABLE IV. Elasticity Estimates for the GDP, Agricultural Exports, and Imports Equations. Pakistan, 1971-90.

	Complete Model Estimated With 3SLS	Exports & Imports Included Estimated With 3SLS	Exports Equation Estimated With 3SLS	Single Equation Models Estimated With OLS
	Model 1	Model 2	Model 3	Model 4
Agricultural Exports equation				
GDP	1.8396***	1.9871***	1.9213***	1.1792**
	(3. 3884)	(3.7820)	(3.5858)	(1.8710)
Net Income Remittances	0. 0533***	0.0532***	0.0532***	0.0533***
	(4.3710)	(4.36%)	(4.3702)	(3.9380)
Investment	− 1.5566***	− 1.6772***	− 1.6234***	− 1.0163*
	(3.0143)	(3.3269)	(3.1744)	(1.7140)
Intercept	− 0.3236	− 0.5123	− 0.4281	0.5216
	(0.3248)	(0.5224)	(0.4324)	(0.4610)
	$R^2 = 0.55$	$R^2 = 0.53$	$R^2 = 0.54$	$R^2 = 0.57$
Imports equation				
GDP	0. 6901*	0.7454**		0.4423
	(1.7606)	(1.9183)		(1.0030)
Net Income Remittances	0.0287***	0.0286***		0.0287***
	(3.3606)	(3.3598)		(3.0270)
Investment	0.6384*	0.5931*		0.8410**
	(1.7260)	(1.6141)		(2.0270)
Intercept	− 1.4348**	− 1.5056**		− 1.1178*
	(2.0270)	(2.1360)		(1.4120)
	$R^2 = 0.82$	$R^2 = 0.82$		$R^2 = 0.82$
GDP equation				
Agricultural Exports	0. 3646***	0.2225***	0.2818***	0.3395***
	(3.7736)	(3.3932)	(4.1430)	(2.818)
Manufactured Exports	0. 5358**		0.2347*	0.6880**
	(2.1394)		(1.5760)	(2.1820)
Imports	− 0.1752	0.1186		− 0.2935
	(1.1038)	(1.1993)		(1.458)
Net Income Remittances	− 0.0106**	− 0.0152**	− 0.0133**	− 0.0048
	(2.0227)	(2.6453)	(2.5986)	(0.7462)
Investment	0.5682***	0.6869***	0.6226***	0.5731***
	(3.8610)	(4.5549)	(3.9712)	(3.1320)
Intercept	1.9342***	0.8934***	1.3608***	2.3435***
	(3.619)	(3.0470)	(3.1170)	(3.5010)
	$R^2 = 0.87$	$R^2 = 0.82$	$R^2 = 0.85$	$R^2 = 0.88$
	System $R^2 = 0.98$	System $R^2 = 0.99$	System $R^2 = 0.97$	

Notes: Figures in parentheses are t-statistics; single asterisks (*), double asterisks (**), and triple asterisks (***) denote significance at 10%, 5%, and 1% levels, respectively.

the hypothesis that agricultural exports generate positive externalities that lead to growth in rest of the economy.

However, when we examine the agricultural export equation (Equation 1), we find that the estimated parameter for GDP growth (while positive and statistically significant at one percent) is much larger than γ_{Xa} was in the previously discussed GDP equation (Equation 3). In all four models this size differential was observed, where the estimated GDP parameter (α_{GDP}) in the agricultural exports equation was anywhere from three and a half to nine times larger than the estimated agricultural export coefficient in the GDP equation. The larger magnitude of α_{GDP} compared to γ_{Xa} may imply that GDP growth has a much larger impact on agricultural export growth than agricultural export growth has on GDP growth.

This relationship between agricultural exports and GDP growth can also be examined in a variety of more indirect manners. To do this we will first evaluate the impact of a shift in export structure away from agriculture exports by examining the effect of manufactured goods share of total exports (X_m) on real per capita GDP. The estimations for all three models which included this variable yielded positive and statistically significantly coefficients. The consistent positive relation suggests that the positive externalities generated by the export sector increase when the share of manufactured goods in total exports increases. This is especially pertinent for the Pakistani economy since such a large percentage of its GDP growth is attributed to industry and manufacturing, relative to its South Asian neighbors.

This study also acknowledged that real per capita GDP might be related to factors such as per capita imports, income remittances, and investment. In order to more fully understand the relationship between agricultural exports and GDP growth, it was necessary to evaluate how these factors affected not only the GDP growth, but also agricultural exports. Starting with the evaluation of the investment parameter in the GDP growth equation, we see reflected in all four models a positive relationship which is statistically significant at a level of one percent. In most cases, this coefficient is larger in magnitude than any other coefficient in the equation. This may imply that an increase in investment leads to more growth in per capita GDP than any other variable.

When we examine the relationship between investment and agricultural exports we find that per capita investment has a statistically significant negative coefficient in all of the equations. The reasons for the negative impact of an increase in investment could be attributable to many factors. It could be indicative of the hypothesis that a net transfer of funds from agriculture to other sectors such as industry may be occurring in the Pakistani economy (Dorosh and Valdes, 1990). It could also be a result of the fact that most domestic industry thrives through the use of agricultural products for inputs. Increased investment in the industrial sector would result in increased domestic demand for agricultural commodities which in turn would decrease the amount of agricultural products available for exports.

The effect of investment on import growth is also examined. The positive sign of the investment coefficient implies that a major part of investment may be spent importing capital goods and technical knowledge from abroad.

When we examine the effect of net foreign income remittances on GPD growth, it is found that in all the models, the coefficient of this variable (γ_{NFI}) is negative. This negative coefficient is not consistent with prior expectations. However, in all four cases the coefficients are very small, implying that an increase in income remittances would have very little effect on GDP. While the effect of income remittances on GDP growth was negative, α_{NFI} was found to be both positive and highly significant in all four models estimating the agricultural exports (equation (1)). These positive coefficients tend to support the hypothesis that income remittances play an indirect role in determining Pakistan's agricultural exports. While NFI allows the country to import pesticides, fertilizers and other inputs for agriculture, it may also result in increased demand for agricultural products and increased investment in the agricultural sector. Increased demand provides incentive for producers to increase their production and the resulting increased supply may increase agricultural exports.

In the imports equation, β_{NFI} was estimated to be positive and statistically significant at a significance level of one percent. The positive impact is consistent with prior expectations, as an increase in net foreign remittances increases foreign exchange availability which is expected to increase imports.

With the results showing that imports are partially determined by income remittance and investment, we now stand prepared to evaluate the relationship between imports and GDP growth. The coefficient of the import variable (γ_M) in the GDP growth equation was expected to have a positive sign, since the increased imports of capital goods and raw materials is expected to increase overall production. This expectation was not reflected in the results, as the coefficient of the real per capita imports was negatively related to the dependent GDP growth variable in both Models 1 and 4. In one of the variations of the 3SLS model (3), this parameter indicates a positive relationship, but in none of the models are the parameters statistically significant. Capital imports account for forty-three percent of total imports into Pakistan (Finance Division, 1992). Since 1970, capital imports for industry have increased from 3,285 million Rupees to 167,815 million Rupees in 1992. With this much of Pakistan's imports consisting of capital goods for industry, imports are likely indicative of industrial expansion. With such large increases in imports of capital goods for industrial expansion, it is difficult to explain the negative coefficient associated with imports in the GDP growth equation. The negative coefficient implies that this particular expansion by the industrial sector may have been related to negative growth in the Pakistani economy. This may indicate support for the hypothesis that Pakistan's capital intensive industries are highly inefficient. Increases in the importation of industrial capital goods would indicate expansion in capital intensive industries. Capital intensive manufacturing begins to compete for limited resources, and governmental policies designed to promote industry allow these inefficient industries to absorb resources which could have been applied to more productive uses. The economy as a whole could be damaged by this type of expansion. In a situation such as this, a negative coefficient for γ_M is highly feasible. However, note that this negative coefficient was not statistically significant.

We also evaluated GDP as an independent variable in the imports equation. The coefficient of per capita GDP was positive in the complete 3SLS model (1), in the variation of this 3SLS model (2), and in the single equation OLS model (4). The coefficient is statistically significant at a significance level of 10 percent in the first model and at a significance level of 5 percent in the second model. The positive sign implies that growth in per capita GDP has allowed the country to increase its imports.

CONCLUSIONS

The primary purpose of this study was to examine the role of agricultural exports on the economic development of Pakistan. Information of this nature is vital for the analysis of economic development strategies in Pakistan. The timing of this information is critical as Pakistan's policy makers now face major economic reforms in their quest for development. As Pakistan's government is put under pressure to alter its historical treatment of agricultural policy, the future of Pakistan's agricultural sector is uncertain. Understanding the impact of agricultural exports on GDP growth provides important information for policy analysts.

The results of this study show that the amount of agricultural goods exported from Pakistan is positively related to Pakistan's economic growth. The results of this study are consistent with the results of other studies related to other developing regions of the world. Svedberg (1993) in a study of several African countries concludes that the decline in agricultural exports was one of the main reasons of economic crisis and sluggish GNP growth. Another study by YAO on China's economic growth suggests a strong relationship between the agricultural sector in general and economic growth. It is further concluded that agriculture is the driving force for all the other economic sectors, even though its share in national income has been falling sharply over time. Moreover the study suggests that the growth in other sectors has had little impact on agricultural incomes.

Another point of interest in this study is that while agricultural exports were shown to have a positive and significant relationship with GDP growth, the magnitude of its coefficient (γ_{Xa}) is smaller than the coefficient of manufactured exports share (γ_{Xm}). This may imply that GDP benefits more from an export structure which is rich in manufactured goods. An empirical study of reallocation of resources in developing countries suggests that transferring labor from the agricultural sector to other sectors of the economy is associated with economic growth (Humphries and Knowles, 1998). This may be because agricultural labor is less productive than labor employed in other sectors of the economy. The study suggests either transferring labor out of agriculture to the industrial or the services sectors, or increasing agricultural labor productivity as two alternatives for increasing the rate of economic growth.

While the results of this study may seem to imply that the economy could benefit by shifting resources from the agricultural sector to the industrial sector in order to better stimulate GDP growth, the matter is not that simple. Other studies have indicated that the growth of the industrial sector is highly related to growth in the agricultural sector (Khan, 1993; Hwa, 1988; Yao, 1996). If this is the case, then the GDP growth examined in this study is expected to be much more dependent on the agricultural sector than can be seen from simply examining the coefficient of agricultural exports in the GDP growth equation. GDP growth is tied to the agricultural sector not only through it's provision of agricultural exports, but also through the stimulation of industrial development which in turn increases the share of manufactured goods in total exports.

Relationships such as this are vital considerations as Pakistan moves to restructure its economy. A thorough understanding of the roles played by all economic sectors is necessary not only for Pakistan, but for all developing nations as they struggle to advance their economies. The agricultural sector is of particular importance due to the traditionally heavy reliance placed upon this sector by the developing world. The results of this study show the impacts of agricultural and manufactured exports, investment, and income remittances on economic growth. In an area of study where much of the previous research simply looked at groups of nations and used models based on economic generalizations, this paper demonstrates the need to study the unique characteristics of a country for understanding the potential impacts of policy decisions.

NOTES

1. Total foreign exchange earnings include earnings from worker's remittances from working abroad. Worker's remittances are a major source of foreign exchange earnings and occupy a significant place in financing the import bill of the country.

2. The domestic resource cost (DRC) estimates have been used to measure comparative advantage. The DRC measures the cost in terms of domestic resources for each dollar earned for exports or for each dollar saved for imported competing goods. Comparative advantage can be measured by dividing the calculated DRC by the accounting exchange rate. If the ratio is less than one, then the country has an advantage in the production of the commodity (Henneberry and Henneberry, 1989)

3. The rice variety developed by the International Rice Research Institute (IRRI).

4. Since the early seventies, Pakistan has been an extensive exporter of labor to the oil rich countries of the Middle East, and the developed world. Pakistan has experienced a significant growth in NFI during the past decades. NFI grew in current prices from 99 million Rupees in 1971 to about 31 billion Rupees in 1990. In constant prices these figures were 319 million Rupees in 1971 and 15 billion Rupees in 1990, respectively.

5. Foreign direct investment (FDI) has been a small but growing part of total investment in Pakistan. Data indicates that FDI in Pakistan has grown from 8 million US dollars in 1976 to 346 million dollars in 1993. During the same period, total gross fixed capital formation grew from 2.4 to 9.2 billion dollars (International Monetary Fund). Nevertheless, excluding the non-capital part, FDI is even a smaller part of total capital formation in Pakistan than these figures reflect.

6. Shazam output gives R^2s for each equation in addition to the system R^2, when the equations are estimated as a system.

AUTHOR NOTE

Dr. Shida Rastegari Henneberry earned her MS and PhD from Iowa State University. She completed a postdoctoral research fellowship at the University of California-Davis. Also, she has served as Assistant Professor of International Trade at Ripon College, Wisconsin. Dr. Henneberry's primary research area is the effect of institutions on market development of agricultural products.

Muhammed E. Khan received his PhD in Agricultural Economics from Oklahoma State University, and is currently a research economist in Pakistan.

REFERENCES

Balassa, B., 1978, "Exports and Economic Growth: Further Evidence," *Journal of Development Economics,* No. 5.

Bandow, D. and I. Vasquez, 1994, *Perpetuating Poverty: The World Bank, the IMF, and the Developing World,* Washington DC: Cato Institute.

Davidson, R. and J.G. McKinnon, 1981, "Several Test for Model Specification in the Presence of Alternative Hypotheses," *Econometrica,* Vol. 49.

Dorosh, P. and A. Valdes, 1990, "Effects of Exchange Rate and Trade Policies on Agriculture in Pakistan," International Food Policy Research Institute, Report No. 84.

Esfahani, H.S., 1991, "Exports, Imports, and Economic Growth in Semi-Industrialized Countries," *Journal of Development Economics,* Vol. 35.

Feder, G., 1983, "On Exports and Economic Growth," *Journal of Development Economics,* Vol. 12.

Finance Division: Government of Pakistan, 1992, *Economic Survey 1991-92,* Islamabad: Government of Pakistan.

Finance Division: Government of Pakistan, 1993, *Economic Survey 1992-93,* Islamabad: Government of Pakistan.

Henneberry, S. and D. Henneberry, 1989. "International Trade Policies," in Luther Tweeten (Ed.) *Agricultural Policy Analysis Tools for Economic Development,* Boulder: Westview Press, pp. 322-354.

Hommond, R. and L. McGowen, 1994, "Ghana: The World Bank's Sham Showcase," in Kevin Danaher (Ed.) *Fifty Years is Enough,* Boston: South End Press.

Humphries, H. and S. Knowles, 1998, "Does Agriculture Contribute to Economic Growth? Some Empirical Evidence," *Applied Economics,* Vol. 30, 775-781.

Hwa, Erh-Cheng, 1988, "The Contribution of Agriculture to Economic Growth: Some Empirical Evidence," *World Development,* Vol. 16, No. 11.

International Monetary Fund (IMF), *International Financial Statistics Yearbook,* Various Issues.

Jung, W.S. and P.J. Marshall, 1985, "Exports Growth and Causality in Developing Countries," *Journal of Development Economics,* Vol. 18.

Khan, M.E., 1993, "Role of Agricultural Sector in Economic and Industrial Growth of Pakistan," Ph.D. Dissertation, Stillwater, OK: Oklahoma State University.

Korten, A., 1994, "Structural Adjustment and Costa Rican Agriculture," in Kevin Danaher (Ed.) *Fifty Years is Enough,* Boston: South End Press.

Ministry of Food and Agriculture: Government of Pakistan, March 1988, *Report of the National Commission on Agriculture,* Islamabad: Government of Pakistan.

Nasim, A. and A. Akhlaque, 1992, "Agricultural Taxation and Subsidies," in *Financing Pakistan's Development in the 90's,* Oxford: Oxford University Press.

Ndaiye, A., 1994, "Food for Thought: Senegal's Struggle with Structural Adjustment," in Kevin Danaher (Ed.) *Fifty Years is Enough,* Boston: South End Press.

Svedberg, P., 1993. "Trade Compression and Economic Decline in Sub-Saharan Africa," in Blomstrom and Lundahl (Ed.) *Economic Crisis in Africa: Perspectives on Policy Responses.* New York: Routlege, pp. 21-40.

Tisch, S. and M. Wallace, 1994, *Dilemmas of Development Assistance,* Boulder, CO: *Westview Press.*

Ty, R., 1994, "Asia," in *Justice Denied,* Kathmandu: INHURED International.

Tyler, W. G., 1981, "Growth and Export Expansion in Developing Countries: Some Empirical Evidence," *Journal of Development Economics,* Vol. 9.

White, K.T., S.D. Wong, D. Whistler, and S.N. Navn, 1993, *Shazam User's Reference Manual,* Version 7.0, New York: McGraw Hill.

Yao, Shujie, 1996, "Sectoral Cointegration, Structural Break and Agricultural's Role in the Chines Economy in 1952-92: A VAR Approach," *Applied Economics,* Vol. 28, 1269-1279.

Ethnic Niche Markets
for Fresh Canadian Pork
in the United States Pacific Northwest

Peter Kuperis
Michel Vincent
James Unterschultz
Michele Veeman

SUMMARY. The ethnic Asian market in Washington and Oregon constitutes a sizable niche market for fresh Canadian pork. The objectives of this study are to evaluate the Asian ethnic markets for fresh pork in the United States Pacific Northwest and Vancouver.

Asian retailers and distributors in Vancouver, Seattle and Portland were surveyed by direct interview during November and December 1996. The survey applied semantic differential scaling questions, open-ended questions and a stated preference task, a conjoint methodology, to examine pork retailer's and distributor's perceptions of fresh pork produced in Western Canada and in the Midwest United States.

The survey results show Western Canadian pork enjoys an image of superior quality amongst retailers and distributors in Seattle's ethnic Asian market. Asian retailers in Portland are less familiar with Western Canadian pork and did not regard it as highly as did retailers in Seattle. Distributors in Portland are more familiar with Western Canadian pork and

Peter Kuperis and Michel Vincent are Research Assistants, James Unterschultz is Assistant Professor and Michele Veeman is Professor, all affiliated with the Department of Rural Economy, University of Alberta.

Address correspondence to: James Unterschultz, Department of Rural Economy, University of Alberta, Edmonton, Alberta, Canada T6G 2H1 (E-mail: jim.unterchultz@ualberta.edu).

[Haworth co-indexing entry note]: "Ethnic Niche Markets for Fresh Canadian Pork in the United States Pacific Northwest." Kuperis, Peter et al. Co-published simultaneously in *Journal of International Food & Agribusiness Marketing* (International Business Press, an imprint of The Haworth Press, Inc.) Vol. 10, No. 4, 1999, pp. 31-45; and: *Cross-National and Cross-Cultural Issues in Food Marketing* (ed: Erdener Kaynak) International Business Press, an imprint of The Haworth Press, Inc., 1999, pp. 31-45. Single or multiple copies of this article are available for a fee from The Haworth Document Delivery Service [1-800-342-9678, 9:00 a.m. - 5:00 p.m. (EST). E-mail address: getinfo@haworthpressinc.com].

consider it to be superior to Midwest United States pork in terms of overall quality, meat color and fat trim. In both markets, Western Canadian pork is generally considered to be expensive. These results are not statistically significant; however, they are of economic relevance since most of the major players in the segment were interviewed. *[Article copies available for a fee from The Haworth Document Delivery Service: 1-800-342-9678. E-mail address: getinfo@haworthpressinc.com <Website: http://www.haworthpressinc.com>]*

KEYWORDS. Ethnic niche markets, Canadian pork, U.S.A. Pacific Northwest, distribution network

INTRODUCTION

Increasingly, food marketers are placing an emphasis on niche markets that consist of an identifiable sub-group of consumers with specific needs or preferences. One such niche market is the "ethnic Asian market" in the United States Pacific Northwest (PNW). The Asian population of Washington and Oregon, two states in the PNW, is projected to increase from 429,000 persons in 1995 to 873,000 persons by the year 2010 (U.S. Department of Commerce, 1996). Pork is an important component of the Asian diet, and is primarily consumed as fresh meat. Thus, the ethnic Asian market in Washington and Oregon constitutes a sizable niche market for fresh Canadian pork. A significant Asian market segment also exists in the greater Vancouver region, a Canadian city located adjacent to the Pacific Northwest of the United States. To capture the market potential of a niche segment, it is necessary to identify particular product or service needs within that market segment, to understand the perceptions held by buyers servicing that market and to evaluate the differences in niche markets in separate locations.

The objectives of this study are to evaluate the Asian ethnic markets for fresh pork in the Pacific Northwest of the United States. The specific objectives are to: (1) evaluate the market for fresh pork in the ethnic Asian market; (2) identify whether there are any perceived quality differences at the retailer and wholesaler level between fresh pork sourced from Canada, versus pork sourced from the U.S. Midwest and (3) compare the ethnic Asian market and its structure in Vancouver, Seattle and Portland. Thus, within this project, we evaluated and compared both cross-cultural demand differences and cross-national differences in a specific ethnic market.

A two-stage process was employed in this study. Initially existing literature was reviewed as were data on market disappearance and export trends. Interviews with Canadian industry experts identified markets for Canadian pork in the Pacific Northwest as a significant potential market segment.

Retailers and meat distributors that cater specifically to the ethnic Asian market were identified as the most suitable target group to survey by direct interview due to their familiarity with fresh pork and potential knowledge about the Asian ethnic market.

Asian retailers and distributors in Vancouver, Seattle and Portland were surveyed by direct interview during November and December 1996. The survey applied semantic differential scaling questions, open-ended questions and a stated preference task, a conjoint methodology, to examine pork retailers' and distributors' perceptions of fresh pork produced in Western Canada and in the Midwest United States. This approach allowed a comparison of the "product image" of pork from these two sources in the ethnic Asian market and also enabled an assessment of the survey methodologies that were applied in the study. The distribution systems in each of the three areas were also assessed and compared. The information on perceptions about pork quality and other product and source characteristics can be used to develop marketing strategies for fresh pork in the market segments. Such information may also aid the evaluation of branding strategies. Other studies such as by Kim et al. (1997), Speece and Maclachlan (1991), Huang and Fu (1995) and Kyriakopoulos and Oude Phuis (1997) have used similar survey techniques to evaluate consumer preferences in international markets.

MARKET BACKGROUND

The Pacific Northwest (Washington and Oregon) is the major export market in the United States for Western Canadian meat packers and this is a particularly important market for fresh pork. In 1995, this region accounted for 56.9 percent of fresh pork and 38.4 percent of processed pork exported to the United States from Western Canada. These were supplied mainly from the Canadian provinces of Alberta and British Columbia (Agriculture and Agri-Food Canada, 1995). The Pacific Northwest (PNW) is an attractive market for Western Canada since the region is highly deficit in pork and Canada has the advantage of close location, giving a significant transportation cost advantage over the Midwest United States in serving Washington and Oregon. There are no explicit trade barriers for pork between Canada and the United States; tariffs on cross-border trade in pork were eliminated in 1991. Nonetheless, border inspections apply and regulations regarding packaging and labeling are not harmonized (Personal communication with Canadian pork packers; MacMillan et al., 1994).

The PNW is an area of rapidly growing population. Seattle and Vancouver are two of the fastest growing metropolitan areas in the United States and Canada (Gale Research, 1993; Statistics Canada, 1996). There is a sizable segment of population in the PNW that has ethnic Asian origins. This is also true for Vancouver which has experienced rapid growth in Asian population, mainly due to immigration from Hong Kong (Agriculture and Agri-Food Canada, 1994). This trend is now tending to moderate. Persons of Chinese origin form the largest Asian ethnic group in Vancouver, while the Asian populations of Seattle and Portland are more diverse. Seattle and Portland have not experienced sizable immigration from Asia in the past few years.

Production and consumption levels of pork in Washington and Oregon in recent years are shown in Tables 1 and 2. In both states the estimated consumption deficit is necessarily filled by interstate shipments and international imports. The large pork deficit of Washington reflects a decrease in pork production in this state of 35 percent from 1988 to 1994, while the estimated consumption of pork increased by 19 percent from 1988 to 1994. Thus, the "self-sufficiency ratio" for pork decreased from 6.9 percent in 1988 to 3.8 percent in 1994. Similar trends underlie the pork deficit of Oregon. Local pork production decreased by 42 percent between 1988 and 1994 and the self-sufficiency ratio declined from 24 percent to 12 percent.

TABLE 1. Total Supply and Disposition of Pork, Washington (Thousand Tonnes[1])

Year	Production	Washington Consumption[2]	Canadian Imports (AB and BC)	Market Share– Western Canada (%)	International Interstate Imports[3]	Total Supply
1988	9.8	141.5	19.7	13.9	112.0	141.5
1989	10.1	143.3	14.8	10.8	117.7	143.3
1990	10.4	141.1	15.9	11.3	114.8	141.1
1991	7.9	147.5	14.8	8.8	126.6	147.5
1992	7.9	159.9	14.6	9.1	137.4	159.9
1993	6.7	167.6	15.5	9.2	145.4	167.6
1994	6.4	168.4	16.6	9.9	145.4	168.4

[1]Carcass weight. [2]Estimate based on United States pork consumption data. [3]Estimate based on columns 1 and 2.
Sources: U.S. Department of Agriculture *Agricultural Statistics* 1988-1995
Alberta Agriculture, Food and Rural Development (1988-1995)

TABLE 2. Supply and Disposition of Pork, Oregon (Thousand tonnes[1])

Year	Production	Washington Consumption[2]	Canadian Imports (AB and BC)	Market Share- Western Canada (%)	International Interstate Imports[3]	Total Supply
1988	20.3	83.6	1.6	1.9	61.7	83.6
1989	18.2	84.3	3.4	4.0	62.7	84.3
1990	14.8	82.4	2.4	2.9	65.2	82.4
1991	12.2	85.8	2.6	3.0	71.0	85.8
1992	12.0	92.1	6.2	6.7	73.9	92.1
1993	11.9	92.8	5.7	6.1	75.2	92.8
1994	11.8	95.7	8.3	8.7	75.6	95.7

[1]Carcass weight. [2]Estimate based on United States pork consumption data. [3]Estimate based on columns 1 and 2.
Sources: Oregon Agriculture and Fisheries Statistics, 1994-1995
U.S. Department of Agriculture, World Livestock Situation, 1992 and Livestock and Poultry:
World Markets and Trade, 1996 U.S. Department of Commerce, 1996
Alberta Agriculture, Food and Rural Development (1988-1995)

Exports of fresh and processed pork from Alberta and British Columbia to the United States increased between 1988 and 1995 by 40 percent, from 36,204 tons to 50,847 tons (Table 3). Exports of fresh pork increased by 22 percent, from 28,253 tons to 34,434 tons, while exports of processed pork increased by 106 percent, from 7,951 tons to 16,413 tons. Washington and Oregon are the main United States market for Western Canadian pork, particularly for fresh pork. In 1995, this region accounted for 56.7 percent of fresh pork and 38.3 percent of processed pork exported from Alberta and British Columbia to the United States (Table 3). California is the other major United States market for pork; Canada has less of a locational advantage for this market (Alberta Agriculture, Food and Rural Development, 1995).

Some features of the PNW market have been changing. Washington used to be a large buyer of fresh Canadian pork but this region is increasingly supplied from the Midwest United States. Canadian shipments of fresh pork to Washington decreased by 50 percent between 1988 and 1995 (Table 3), although shipments of processed pork remained steady. However, Canadian shipments of fresh pork to Oregon rose by 1,113 percent over this time period and shipments of processed pork more than doubled (Table 3).

SURVEY METHODOLOGY

The survey applied three types of questions: quantitative scaling questions, qualitative questions and stated preference questions to evaluate the attitudes of the target group of retailers and distributors towards fresh pork. Using the semantic differential scales approach, respondents were asked to rate a particular attribute on a seven-level semantic differential scale relative to two broad bipolar adjectives. The semantic differential scale has been used by Nagashima (1970), Papadopoulos et al. (1994) and Kim et al. (1996). The approach allows researchers to examine both the direction and intensity of respondents' attitudes towards such concepts as corporate image, advertising

TABLE 3. Exports of Pork from Western Canada to the Pacific Northwest of the United States (Tonnes[1])

Year	Washington Fresh	Washington Processed	Oregon Fresh	Oregon Processed	PNW Percent Fresh	PNW Percent Processed	Total U.S. Fresh	Total U.S. Processed
1988	14,920	4,754	1,007	559	56.4	66.8	28,253	7,951
1989	9,844	4,947	2,763	604	58.9	65.0	21,390	8,546
1990	10,390	5,553	1,810	555	36.3	56.5	33,597	10,848
1991	9,182	5,642	2,102	451	33.3	48.2	33,893	12,646
1992	8,534	6,060	5,951	244	49.6	41.8	29,212	15,070
1993	8,313	7,155	5,444	212	51.8	38.1	26,570	19,344
1994	8,790	7,838	7,859	490	59.3	43.9	28,060	18,978
1995	7,323	4,806	12,212	1,476	56.7	38.3	34,434	16,413

[1]Carcass weight.
Source: Alberta Agriculture, Food and Rural Development (1988-1995)

image, brand or service image, and country image (Green, Tull and Albaum, 1988). For example, a respondent can be asked to rate the price of a product on a scale of -3 to $+3$, with -3 representing "expensive" and $+3$ representing "inexpensive." In designing a semantic differential scale task, the selection of an appropriate sample of adjective pairs is central to the ability to generate a score for the attribute and product being examined (Churchill, 1991). The product can then be compared to other products using this score. Nagashima (1970) views semantic differential scales to be an effective tool in cross-cultural and cross-linguistic settings.

Two groups of semantic differential questions were used. One set of nine questions focused on product quality evaluation for such features as price, fat color, meat color, food safety and water content. The second set of questions focused on promotion and service-assistance. The choice of product quality factors was based on results from the initial interviews with industry experts and Asian retailers in Western Canada. To prevent sequence bias and response routinization, the semantic differential scale was randomly rotated (Papadopoulos et al. 1994).

The qualitative portion of the survey included a set of structured, open-ended questions. The grocers and distributors who buy pork for sale to Asian consumers were asked for their opinions regarding the main fresh pork attributes that influence Asian pork buyers, the marketing and distribution of fresh pork, the origin and branding of fresh pork, the future of the ethnic "Asian fresh pork market" and the specific pork cuts demanded in these markets. Color pictures of the various cuts provided by the Canadian pork industry (Agriculture and Agri-Food Canada, Canada Pork International) were used to describe potential cuts.

Stated preference questions are an extension of conjoint analysis (Adamowicz et al., 1994; Unterschultz et al., 1997). These questions involved a formal statistical design to evaluate respondents' stated responses to attributes of price, freshness, country of origin and type of cut. The stated preference approach uses statistical models to measure the probability of choice based on different product attribute levels. Each respondent answered eight related choice questions. Each question gave the respondent a written description of two different pork products. Price, product freshness, fat color, type of meat cut, meat color and country of origin were varied between the questions. Multinomial legit models were used to analyze the data. The multinomial model estimates the probability of a respondent choosing a particular product. Positive coefficients on an attribute such as freshness reflect the increased probability of the respondent choosing the fresh product. Negative coefficients indicate the decreased probability of a respondent choosing a product.

The field work was carried out during November and December of 1996 in Seattle and Portland and a similar study of the comparable market segment in

Vancouver was also conducted. Respondents were selected according to geographic location, by referral through local packers and with the assistance of Asian business and cultural organizations in Vancouver and in Seattle. Vancouver respondents include eight Asian retailers and two meat distributors; these constitute the major traders in this ethnic Asian market, in which consumers are mainly of Chinese origin. In addition, open-ended interviews were conducted with two meat packers. In Seattle, respondents included seven Asian retailers, three meat distributors, and one packer-wholesaler. Additional open-ended interviews were conducted with one Canadian consular official and one meat packer sales representative. Portland respondents included eight Asian retailers, three meat distributors or wholesalers, one broker, one packer-wholesaler, and one retailer-wholesaler. In Portland and Seattle, customers in the ethnic Asian market are not primarily of Chinese origin. In each city the respondents represented the major portion of the target population of distributors and retailers in each of the three niche markets. The structure of the target market in each location was documented and compared.

SURVEY RESULTS

Market Structure Description

The structure of the market for fresh pork represented by retailers catering to Asian consumers in Vancouver differs from that in Seattle and Portland. The "Asian market" in Vancouver is dominated by many small shops although a new type of retailer, the "Chinese supermarket," also appears to be gaining prominence in this market. Most of the retailers that specialize in sales to Asian consumers deal directly with the packers and there are very few distributors or wholesalers of pork that are active in this market. Retailers in this market segment purchase fresh pork sides directly from packers located in the Vancouver area. The pork is processed by custom cutting into large cuts in the store.

Seattle's ethnic Asian market is also dominated by many small shops. Retailers in Seattle deal with a variety of suppliers of fresh pork, including packers, wholesalers, brokers and distributors. The Seattle retailers purchase fresh pork as prime cuts and process these in the store. These retailers purchase the standard prime cuts and did not express a preference for any "specialty" cuts.

Retailers specializing in Asian customers in Portland purchase fresh pork from distributors, brokers, wholesalers and a packer-wholesaler. Asian retailers in Portland purchase fresh pork as prime cuts and process these in the store. As in Seattle, these retailers purchase the standard prime cuts and did not express a preference for any "specialty" cuts.

Formal Survey Results
for the Qualitative and Semantic Scale Approaches by City

Results for Vancouver

The United States exports minimal quantities of pork to the Vancouver region. Thus all results for the Vancouver market relate only to Canadian pork. The responses to the open-ended questions identified meat color, fat trim and price as the most important attributes of fresh pork. Table 4 shows that color of Western Canadian pork was rated as acceptable at 1.40 under the semantic scaling (the best score possible is 3.0). Retailers catering to Asian consumers prefer pork with a bright red color which serves as an indicator of freshness in this market. The fat trim of current supplies was rated as acceptable by retailers in Vancouver (Table 4), although some of these retailers indicated that they desire pork with even less outside fat than is currently available from the packers. Price received a negative rating in the semantic differential scale, indicating that the retailers perceived Western Canadian pork to be expensive. This segment of Vancouver retailers indicated that they were satisfied with the service and assistance they received from packers. No distributors were surveyed in Vancouver.

Results for Seattle

Seattle retailers identified fat trim, price and meat color as the most important attributes of fresh pork, similar to Vancouver respondents. Western Canadian pork was rated higher than Midwest United States pork for overall quality (Table 5). Asian retailers in Seattle regard Western Canadian pork as considerably leaner than pork from the Midwest United States. Western Canadian pork and Midwest United States pork were considered to be equally

TABLE 4. Quantitative Semantic Differential Scale Results on Product Quality and Promotional Activity for Pork, Vancouver (Retailers and Distributors)

Attributes	Western Canadian Pork[1]	N[2]
Overall pork quality	1.60	10
Meat color	1.40	10
Fat color	1.90	10
Fat trim	1.50	10
Food safety standards	1.33	9
Water content	1.20	10
Price	− 1.60	10
Variety of cuts	1.30	10
Consistency of each shipment	1.40	10
Service and Assistance	1.80	10
Awareness of promotion	0.30	10

[1]Mean rating scores on a scale from − 3 to + 3 with higher scores deemed better.
[2]The number of respondents to each question.

TABLE 5. Quantitative Semantic Differential Scale Results on Product Quality and Promotional Activity for Pork, Seattle

Attributes	Retailers				Distributors			
	Western Canada[1]	N[2]	Midwest U.S.[1]	N[2]	Western Canada[1]	N[2]	Midwest U.S.[1]	N[2]
Overall pork quality	2.75	4	1.30	5	1.67	3	1.20	5
Meat color	2.50	4	1.82	6	1.67	3	1.40	5
Fat color	2.00	4	1.09	6	1.33	3	0.20	5
Fat trim	2.00	4	0.73	6	1.33	3	1.60	5
Food safety standards	1.50	2	1.78	4	0.67	3	1.40	5
Water content	2.00	4	2.18	6	1.67	3	2.00	5
Price	−1.00	4	−0.09	6	−1.33	3	0.40	5
Variety of cuts	1.25	4	1.45	6	1.00	3	2.00	5
Consistency of each Shipment	3.00	4	1.27	6	1.33	3	0.60	5
Service and Assistance	3.00	4	1.10	5	0.67	3	0.00	5
Awareness of promotion	−0.25	4	−0.45	6	−1.00	3	−0.20	5

[1]Mean rating scores on a scale from −3 to +3 with higher scores deemed better.
[2]The number of respondents to each question.

acceptable in terms of meat color and this is also represented in similar scaling results (Table 5). Western Canadian pork was perceived to be more expensive than pork produced in the Midwestern United States. Western Canadian pork received high ratings for both service and consistency of each shipment. Those retailers that dealt with Western Canadian packers were pleased with the service the packers provided and the consistency of the pork they received. Western Canadian pork was also seen as being superior to Midwest United States pork in terms of its overall quality. Retailers catering to Asian consumers were unaware of promotional activities carried out by either the United States or Western Canadian pork industries and this was confirmed by the scaling results (Table 5).

Distributors in Seattle also considered fat trim, price and meat color to be important. Midwest United States pork had a higher rating for fat trim (1.60 versus 1.33) while Western Canadian pork received a higher rating for meat color (1.67 versus 1.40) (Table 5). However fat trim and meat color of pork from both sources were rated as acceptable. Western Canadian pork was perceived to be more expensive than Midwest United States pork. Western Canadian pork was considered superior to Midwest United States pork in terms of overall pork quality. This perception was less pronounced among distributors than it was amongst retailers. Western Canada was seen as not providing as wide a variety of cuts as was available from Midwest United States packers. Distributors were generally unaware of promotional activity carried out by the Western Canadian pork industry and had limited awareness of promotional activity for United States pork.

Results for Portland

Retailers in Portland also identified price, meat color and fat trim as the most important attributes of fresh pork. Western Canadian and Midwest United States pork were not perceived to be expensive, and Western Canadian pork was seen as the least expensive of these. While both types of pork were rated as having acceptable meat color (Table 6), Midwestern United States pork was perceived to have superior meat color to Western Canadian pork. Western Canadian pork was perceived as leaner (i.e. having a closer fat trim) than Midwest United States pork. Retailers in Portland were unaware of promotional activity for either United States or Western Canadian pork. It should be noted that the majority of Asian retailers interviewed in Portland were unfamiliar with Western Canadian pork.

Distributors in Portland identified price, meat color and fat trim as important attributes. Distributors perceived both Midwest United States and Western Canadian pork as expensive, with Western Canadian pork being viewed as the more expensive (Table 6). Western Canadian pork was considered to be superior to Midwest United States pork in terms of meat color and fat trim. Distributors rated Western Canadian pork to be superior to Midwest pork for overall quality. This perception is opposite to that stated by Portland's Asian retailers. The discrepancy may reflect the greater familiarity of distributors than retailers with Western Canadian pork. Only three retailers in Portland were able to rate Western Canadian pork while all six of the distributors interviewed were able to rate pork from Western Canada. Western Canada's pork suppliers were rated similar to Midwest suppliers for service and lower than the Midwest on awareness of promotional activity. Distributors in Port-

TABLE 6. Quantitative Semantic Differential Scale Results on Product Quality and Promotional Activity for Pork, Portland

Attributes	Retailers				Distributors			
	Western Canada[1]	N[2]	Midwest U.S.[1]	N[2]	Western Canada[1]	N[2]	Midwest U.S.[1]	N[2]
Overall pork quality	1.33	3	2.00	6	2.67	6	0.83	6
Meat color	1.33	3	2.12	8	2.00	6	1.33	6
Fat color	0.67	3	2.00	8	1.67	6	1.50	6
Fat trim	2.67	3	1.12	8	2.00	6	0.33	6
Food safety standards	2.00	3	1.50	8	0.60	5	1.00	6
Water content	3.00	2	2.14	7	1.67	6	1.50	6
Price	1.67	3	0.62	8	−1.00	5	−0.33	6
Variety of cuts	0.00	3	0.37	8	1.00	5	1.83	6
Consistency of each Shipment	0.67	3	1.14	7	1.50	6	0.83	6
Service and Assistance	−0.67	3	1.25	8	1.00	5	1.33	6
Awareness of promotion	−1.33	3	−1.12	8	−0.83	6	1.00	6

[1]Mean rating scores on a scale from −3 to +3 with higher scores deemed better.
[2]The number of respondents to each question.

land were unaware of Western Canadian promotional activity but were aware of promotional activity by the United States pork industry.

Results of the Stated Preference Approach

Only fourteen respondents, twelve of them brokers-distributors, answered this part of the survey, which provided us with 112 data points. The aggregated data from Seattle, Portland and Vancouver is presented here due to the small sample size (Table 7). The positive coefficient estimates shown in the table indicate an increasing probability of choice, while negative coefficients indicate a decreased probability of choice, by respondents, of any product with that attribute level. For example, a positive coefficient on a product described as originating from Western Canada increases the probability of that pork product being chosen over a similar pork product that originates in the Midwest U.S. The difference in product origin is significant in this small sample and indicates that Canadian pork is preferred by the broker-distributors surveyed in the study. Price is apparently not an important factor to pork buyers at the broker-distributor level, since none of the estimated coefficients on price are significant. A possible explanation for this finding is that brokers

TABLE 7. Estimated Coefficients on Variables Predicting Choice, Stated Preference Methodology[1]

Variables	Estimated Coefficient	Standard Error
Price:		
Same as last price paid	− 0.035	0.291
10% less than last price paid	− 0.059	0.293
20% less than last price paid	− 0.088	0.266
10% more than last price paid	0.182	0.278
Days From Slaughter:		
8 days	− 0.738*	0.309
6 days	0.446	0.291
4 days	0.202	0.280
2 days	0.090	0.272
Fat Color:		
Yellow	− 0.455*	0.174
White	0.455*	0.174
Type of Cut:		
Sides	− 0.408*	0.165
Prime cut	0.408*	0.165
Meat Color:		
Dark	0.142	0.294
Normal	1.004*	0.279
Extremely dark	− 0.896*	0.308
Pale	− 0.250	0.278
Pork Origin:		
Midwest US	− 0.345*	0.169
Western Canada	0.345*	0.169
Pseudo R^2	0.180	

[1]The total number of respondents is 14. Each respondent answered 8 questions, giving a total of 112 observations.
*Indicates significance at the 95% confidence level.

are particularly concerned with margins, so that the difference between purchase and selling prices is more important to them than the absolute price levels.

Buyers do not prefer hogs that have been slaughtered eight days earlier, suggesting the importance of freshness of pork products. Products over six days old are less likely to be purchased. Coefficient estimates for hogs slaughtered earlier than six days ago all have positive signs and are not statistically significant. However, broker-distributors are concerned if the product is eight days from slaughter. Regarding fat color, buyer-distributors show a positive preference for white-colored fat and a negative reaction to yellow-colored fat. Canadian pork tends to have whiter colored fat due to the use of feed barley in pig rations and this may give Canadian pork an advantage over a competing product from the U.S., which does not have quite the same color of fat. Similarly the significant positive significant coefficient on the type of cuts shows that buyer-distributors prefer prime cuts over side cuts. This result is driven by the responses in the PNW market which purchases prime cuts rather than sides. It is encouraging that even with such a small sample size, the results confirm many of the major conclusions that were derived using the semantic differential scaling questions and the qualitative questions.

This project applied the three types of survey questions of semantic differential scales, stated preference and open-ended questions. All three types of questions were used to assess the importance of various attributes of fresh pork to Asian pork buyers. Two of the methods, semantic differential scales and open-ended questions, proved most useful in this task. The semantic differential questions worked very well in interviews with Asian retailers. These interviews were usually conducted in the store. The semantic differential questions were suited to this busy environment and were easily applied in this cross-cultural and cross-linguistic setting. The open-ended questions also worked well in this environment. The respondents were knowledgeable about the attributes of fresh pork and about their market. Thus, they were able to provide ratings of and opinions about fresh pork attributes. However, the semantic differential scale question dealing with service and assistance from packers was not sufficiently specific to provide useful guidance. Any future study should frame such a question to deal specifically with the frequency and timing of deliveries and the reliability of supply.

While the stated preference approach worked well with distributors, these questions proved to be unsuitable in the interviews with Asian retailers. Stated preference questions require a quiet atmosphere and more concentration than was available in the retail store environment.

As with all personal interview methods, there is the possibility of an "interviewer effect" during the questioning. That is, some of the ratings and responses may have been given in an effort to please the interviewer. There is no valid way of reliably evaluating this potential bias from this particular sample; however, the interviewers were of the opinion that the bias was small.

CONCLUSIONS AND IMPLICATIONS

Western Canadian pork enjoys an image of superior quality amongst retailers and distributors in Seattle's ethnic Asian market. However, this advantage may be insufficient to assure sales in some regions, either because the quality of Midwest United States pork has improved or due to buyers' lack of knowledge. Asian retailers in Portland are less familiar with Western Canadian pork and did not regard this product as highly as did retailers in Seattle. Distributors in Portland are more familiar with Western Canadian pork and consider this to be superior to pork from the Midwest United States in terms of overall quality, meat color and fat trim. In both markets, Western Canadian pork is generally considered to be expensive. Asian retailers and distributors in the Pacific Northwest are unaware of promotional activity carried out by the Western Canadian pork industry. These results are not statistically significant, however they are of economic relevance since most of the major players in the segment were interviewed.

Western Canadian pork presently enjoys a reputation for superior quality amongst the retailers that specialize in sales to Asian consumers in Seattle. This opinion is also held by distributors in this market segment in Portland. However it is also clear that many members of the trade lack information or experience with Canadian pork. If the potential for increased sales to this market segment is to be achieved, more information and education regarding Western Canadian pork to Asian pork buyers and consumers in the Pacific Northwest will be required.

Price is very important to Asian retailers and distributors. The quantitative results show that respondents consider Western Canadian pork to be more expensive than Midwest pork. Consequently one competitive strategy for Western Canadian pork producers and packers is to maintain quality while improving the productivity of hog operations and the efficiency of pork packing plants.

Asian retailers in Vancouver prefer to purchase sides of pork. This reflects a difference in the structure of this market relative to the Asian markets for pork in the Pacific Northwest of the United States. In Vancouver, many small specialty meat shops cater to the ethnic Asian market. Seattle and Portland do not have these specialized meat shops. Asian retailers and distributors in Seattle and Portland prefer to purchase primel cuts. In contrast, Asian retailers in Vancouver deal directly with meat packers. Distributors play a small role in Vancouver's retail market. Asian retailers in Seattle deal with a variety of suppliers, including both packers and distributors. In Portland, retailers catering to Asian consumers trade mainly with distributors and a local packer-wholesaler.

The results of this study clearly demonstrate that ethnic Asian markets in geographically similar locations are not the same. The retail market structure and the type of cut demanded in Vancouver is distinctly different than in the ethnic Asian market segments in Seattle and Portland. Suppliers targeting these market segments must be aware of these differences and should follow different market strategies for Seattle and Portland than for Vancouver.

REFERENCES

Adamowicz, W.L., Louviere, J.J. and Williams, M. (1994). Combining Revealed and Stated Preference Methods for Valuing Environmental Amenities. *Journal of Environmental Economics and Management.* 26: 271-292.

Agriculture and Agri-Food Canada. *Livestock Market Review.* Various issues from 1988 to 1995.

Agriculture and Agri-Food Canada. (1994) *An Assessment of Selected Ethnic Food Markets in Canada.* Market and Industry Services Branch.

Agriculture and Agri-Food Canada. *Pork Quality: A Guide to Understand Color and Structure of Pork Muscle.* Publication 5180/B. Unknown Date.

Alberta Agriculture, Food and Rural Development. *Imports-Exports.* Market Analysis and Statistics Branch, unpublished data, 1988-1995.

Canada Pork International (1991). Canadian Pork Buyers Manual. Ottawa, Canada.

Churchill, Gilbert A. (1991). *Marketing Research: Methodological Foundations.* 5th ed. Dryden Press. Chicago.

Gale Research Inc. (1993) *Statistical Record of Asian Americans.* Gale Research Inc.

Green, Paul E. Tull, Donald S., Albaum, Gary. *Research for Marketing Decisions.* Prentice Hall. N.J. (1988).

Huang, C.L. and Fu, J. (1995). Conjoint Analysis of Consumer Preferences and Evaluation of a Processed Meat. *Journal of International Food and Agribusiness Marketing.* 7 (1): 35-53.

Kim Bo Young, Renee, Unterschultz, J.R, Veeman, M., and Jelen, Paul. (1996). Analysis of the Korean Beef Market: A Study of Hotel Buyers' Perspectives of Beef Imports from Three Major Sources. *Agribusiness* 13 (4): 445-455.

Kyriakopoulos, K. and Oude Ophuis, P.A.M. (1997). A Pre-Purchase Model of Consumer Choice of Biological Foodstuff. *Journal of International Food and Agribusiness Marketing.* 8 (4): 37-53.

Macmillan, J.B. Chorney and Richmond, R. (1994). "Red Meat Forum Project." Department of Agricultural Economics and Farm Management, University of Manitoba, Winnipeg, March.

Nagashima, A. (1970). "A Comparison of Japanese and U.S. Attitudes Towards Foreign Products. *Journal of Marketing.* 34 (1): 68-74.

Papadopoulos, N. and Heslop, L.A. (1994) "An International Comparative Analysis of Consumer Attitudes Towards Canada and Canadian Products." *Canadian Journal of Administrative Sciences.* 11 (3): 224-39.

Speece, M. and Machlachlan, D.L. (1991). "Measurement of Milk Container Preference." *Journal of International Food and Agribusiness Marketing.* 3 (1): 43-64.

Statistics Canada. (1996). *Quarterly Demographic Statistics.* Cat 91-002.

U.S. Department of Commerce. (1996) *Statistical Abstract of the United States.* Economics and Statistics Administration.

Unterschultz, J., Quagrainie, K. and Vincent, M. (1997). Evaluating Quebec's Preference for Alberta Beef Versus US Beef. *Agribusiness.* 13 (5): 457-468.

Quality Policy and Consumer Behavior: The Case of Beef in Spain

J. Briz
M. Mahlau
E. Gutierrez

SUMMARY. A broad view of the European Union (EU) quality policy to the meat sector is given in this article. It analyses the links between quality policy and consumer attitudes and behavior in the Spanish meat market. Quality programs allow traceability within the chain, which is an important improvement, compared to the traditional way of marketing meat. For this reason, we study the evolution and performance of Spanish meat market from the view of consumer behavior. This paper mentions some basic information in quality policies in Spain, including the results of a survey carried out in 1997, with some practical conclusions. *[Article copies available for a fee from The Haworth Document Delivery Service: 1-800-342-9678. E-mail address: getinfo@haworthpressinc.com <Website: http://www.haworthpressinc.com>]*

KEYWORDS. Quality policy, consumer behavior, Spain, beef, competition, quality, attributes, consumer policy, communications

INTRODUCTION

Quality Policy in relation to consumer behavior is a very timely topic, since the consumer is the final link in the food chain. In a competitive market,

---

J. Briz, M. Mahlau, and E. Gutierrez are affiliated with Polytechnic University of Madrid, E.T.S. Ingenieros Agrónomos, 28040 Madrid, Spain.

This article is part of the Project "Quality Policy and Consumer Behavior" sponsored by the E.U. FAIR-CT 95-0046

[Haworth co-indexing entry note]: "Quality Policy and Consumer Behavior: The Case of Beef in Spain." Briz, J., M. Mahlau and E. Guitierrez. Co-published simultaneously in *Journal of International Food & Agribusiness Marketing* (International Business Press, an imprint of The Haworth Press, Inc.) Vol. 10, No. 4, 1999, pp. 47-62; and: *Cross-National and Cross-Cultural Issues in Food Marketing* (ed: Erdener Kaynak) International Business Press, an imprint of The Haworth Press, Inc., 1999, pp. 47-62. Single or multiple copies of this article are available for a fee from The Haworth Document Delivery Service [1-800-342-9678, 9:00 a.m. - 5:00 p.m. (EST). E-mail address: getinfo@haworthpressinc.com].

farmers,' processors' and retailers' objectives should meet consumer demands.

A traditional approach of the EU quality policy is oriented to the product. In recent years, the EUROP classification of meat has been introduced as a regulation concerning aspects of process-oriented quality policy. However, the consumer-oriented quality approach will dominate the discussion of food quality in the future.

The Reform of the Common Agricultural Policy (CAP) takes in consideration "the increased importance of quality products and the consequent introduction of rules (geographical indications, certificates of specific character) and the key issues affect consumer behavior, consumer attitudes and acceptability, implications of new technologies on consumer confidence, improved understanding of food choice, environmental and ethical aspects, socio-economic factors, access and availability and, finally, communication and information flow to consumers, retailers, manufacturers, and primary producers" (C. Becker et al., 1997, p. 1).

There is an effort at the European Union to harmonize the legislation of the member states, and to adopt rules under the Protection of Geographical Indications (PGI) and Designation of Origin (PDO), besides the quality control systems according to ENISO 9000-9004.

All this institutional effort has to be complemented with a dynamic position of all the economic participants along the food chain. Finally, the results will depend upon the acceptance of consumers.

As an integrated part of the European market, the Spanish segment shares the main objectives:

(a) Identification of consumer expectations of meat quality and of how the products fulfill those expectations.
(b) Identification of factors determining the success or failure in managing quality at the meat production chain.
(c) Identification of potential mechanisms to increase meat consumption.

As in other European countries, quality policy has become increasingly important in Spain. Farmer organizations and the meat industry are trying to regain the consumer's confidence in fresh meat quality due to increasing concerns regarding BSE and hormones in meat.

The EU has supported the National Quality Programs, paying special attention to the consumer's opinion. For these reasons, all the partners involved in the meat chain are interested in getting information about the existing different meat quality programs and consumer attitudes and purchasing behavior regarding meat products.

Good knowledge of the meat sector is a basic instrument for policy makers and private entrepreneurs, in order to satisfy the consumers. Sources of information should include national statistical data and literature complemented with further empirical work.

In this article, we try to analyze consumers' habits and possible responses to quality policies surveyed by public and private institutions. After a brief comment of the methodology, there are general descriptions of quality attributes and policies in relation to consumer behavior. Analysis of the results of the survey is mentioned in the specific scenario of the meat market.

METHODOLOGY

The increasing market competition at the European market requires the development of efficient marketing strategies. In this framework, a basic understanding of consumer behavior is the key to entrepreneurial success.

According to R. Alvensleben (1997), consumer behavior is very complex, and the theory of analysis is a multidisciplinary interaction of different disciplines, such as economics, sociology, nutrition, psychology and anthropology. Consumer behavior consists of three basic points: the emotion, the attitude and the motivation. The way the actions take place is, firstly, the influence the emotion causes to the motivation. Then, the attitude and finally the behavior.

Enterprises involved in the food chain depend on consumers' perception of their products (K. Grunert et al. 1997). The analysis of consumers' value perception may be done at an aggregate or at an individual level, and the goals are different at both situations. At an aggregate level, the information may be useful to understand consumer behavior in a certain market and to design the marketing strategies in order to increase the purchases. We should also compare consumers from different markets and varied cultures and analyze market trends. In both cases, information may help to develop strategies and to allocate resources.

Studies of consumers at an individual level may help to understand the concept and perception of quality, that is, the trade-off between quality and price.

Food safety is becoming a major concern in the consumer's attitude (Senauer 1991), that may become a widespread alarm. However, there is a certain resistance to change unhealthy food habits due to tradition. Many consumers agree on eating a healthier diet as long as there are not significant changes in their consumption patterns. Therefore, there is a potential market for food products that change nutritional characteristics but maintain sensory attributes (taste, flavor, etc.). In some way, it gives more opportunity to traditional or local products but with some changes: low or non-fat, low or no cholesterol, low calorie intake. This is the main reason of why white meat is more appreciated than red meat, and so is leaner meat.

In this broad scenery, we focus our attention on some basic points, the attributes, and the quality policy performed by the Spanish institutions, their connection with the agricultural policy, and the relationship between these aspects and the consumer's behavior.

We are certainly concerned about the complexity of the task, but our main goal is to call attention to the importance of consumer behavior, as an orientation of the whole activity in the food chain. In the case of the meat sector, there is clear evidence of the importance of food safety. The BSE in beef has been a significant event, with a clear reaction of consumer attitudes, substitution effects in the meat market and development of quality policies and trade control.

Enterprises are looking for a way to be competitive, that is to create a higher value to the consumer's eyes than other competitors, or to supply products with similar value at a lower price. The consumer's value perception has been analyzed by some theories, such as means-end chain, trying to associate product attributes, relevant consequences and personal values. Thus, a product attribute is relevant when it may lead to some consequences to the consumer's final decision. A model elaborated by Grunert et al. (1993) identifies several aspects of the consumer's value perception: the relation between the desired consequences and personal values, certain abstract values, concern attributes, shopping and meal preparation instructions, and usage situation.

What we show here in this work is a preliminary step, setting the basis to a further analysis, and trying to identify consumers from different market segments.

Consumers' health considerations may explain some significant changes at the European meat market. Thus, market share of poultry is growing although prices have raised since 1970 (Nielsen 1998). Consumers try to avoid red meat and saturated fat content. An ER survey in 15 ER member states and 15,000 respondents shows that 17% of them described "healthy eating" as "eating less red meat and more chicken and fish." Also 40% of the respondents mentioned "eating less fat" (IEJS 1996, mentioned by Nielsen).

Another survey of nine thousand consumers showed that an ideal food product should have the following attributes: "healthy" (63%), "no harmful substances" (57%) and "natural" (53%). Other factors, such as "tasty" (18%) and "not expensive" were less important (Splitters 1993).

In this article we try to describe the situation in the Spanish meat market, based on national reports using available literature and national statistical database (Furitsch 1994). Later on, there was an empirical work, designing and executing a consumer survey (conducting test-interviews, final interviews and additional in-depth interviews). Other sources were the Spanish Ministry of Agriculture, Fishery and Food and professional institutions, especially the collaboration with ASOCARNE.

As we mentioned above, this work tries to identify the link between quality policy and consumer behavior in the Spanish meat sector. The empirical data are based on a random sample of 500 telephone inquiries at a national level. A parallel survey was made with the same methodology in five other countries during 1997 in the frame of the European project "EU FAIR CT 9500-46" (Briz et al. 1998).

Table 1 shows the details of the characteristics of the sample and the structure of the Spanish population. We have considered only a part of the population, that is, people who are responsible for the shopping in house-

TABLE 1. Summary of Social and Demographic Data.

%	Characteristics	Survey	National
Sex	☐ Female	88.8	50.8
	☐ Male	11.2	49.2
Age A	☐16-29		27.8
	☐ 30-39		16.7
	☐ 40-49		15.0
	☐ 50-59		13.2
	☐ 60 and over		27.3
Age B	☐ Under 30	15.3	41.2
	☐ 30-39	27.6	13.6
	☐ 40-49	28.3	12.2
	☐ 50-59	21.7	10.8
	☐ 60 and over	8.1	22.2
Household size	☐ 1 person	4.6	14.4
	☐ 2 people	18.8	21.8
	☐ 3 people	22.4	21.0
	☐ 4 people	28.8	26.1
	☐ 5 people	16.8	10.9
	☐ 6 people or more	8.6	5.8
	Average		3.2
Children under 16	☐ No children	59.2	53.4
	☐ 1 child	22.8	18.2
	☐ 2 children	14.0	17.8
	☐ 3 children	3.2	7.3
	☐ 4 or more children	0.8	3.4
	Average		1.9
Age when stopped full-time education	☐ < 15 years	45.0	64.0
	☐ 15-18 years	27.2	18.9
	☐ More than 18 years	27.8	16.2
	Average age		15.4
Occupation of the respondents	☐ Housewife	60.2	
	☐ Retired	6.0	
	☐ Others not working	7.5	
	☐ Self employed	7.9	
	☐ Employed professional or management	7.1	
	☐ Other employed position	11.3	
Occupation of person who contributes most to the household income	☐ Housewife	2.0	31.7
	☐ Retired	18.8	11.0
	☐ Others not working	4.8	17.13
	☐ Self employed	29.4	7.4
	☐ Employed professional or management	16.4	6.5
	☐ Other employed position	28.7	26.1

holds and who have a telephone at home. Approximately 77% of the Spanish households have a telephone. Therefore, there are some differences between the sample and the population.

In this way, the following aspects have been analyzed: meat consumption, quality perception, consumer reactions, labels, brands, and trust.

On the other hand, the quality policy within the meat sector has been analyzed using both secondary and primary sources of information, in order to compare what the industry offers to the consumer demands. In Spain, people usually consume fresh meat.

The share of frozen meat in total meat consumption is very low in beef and veal (2.7%), pork (2.9%) and poultry (2.5%) (INE 1994). Therefore, this article only deals with fresh meat.

QUALITY ATTRIBUTES AND CONSUMER BEHAVIOR

Farmers or industries and their associations have initiated a great part of the quality programs in the Spanish meat sector. Special institutions (Consejos Reguladores) have been created for assessing each scheme. Retailers or butchers have established parallel programs based in their own brand, and some of them sell quality meat from the generic programs. Public institutions (EU, national, regional) have an important influence in the regulation, implementation and promotion of quality programs. At the beginning, these programs were often initiated by regional or national institutions, but the European institutions are becoming more and more important.

Among the reasons for quality policy in Spain, we should mention the decrease of profitability of livestock production and marketing, and the support of many programs by many agents of the supply chain, a loss of confidence in the healthfulness of beef and veal (or other meat) by many consumers due to published reports about topics like growth enhancers, BSE and cholesterol. In any case there is an increasing demand for transparency and quality control at the consumer level in order to assure meat quality.

Other aspects are the willingness to pay higher prices for controlled meat by many consumers (at present, prices are some 10-17% higher than for "not certified" meat), and a decentralization of Spanish agricultural policy in parallel with the Common Agricultural Policy (CAP) of the EU (European Quality Beef, IGP, DPO, etc.).

At present, the production and marketing of beef and veal within quality programs are increasing with high growth rates, but the share of this type of meat and of traceability in the supply chain is low (some 5%). Spain probably will not adopt the EU regulations in the first step, and will delay their application due to inadequate organization.

The main instruments for quality policy are national quality schemes, retailer quality schemes, and quality management systems (like ISO). Most of these instruments are voluntary, but some are mandatory. They assure quality control along the whole supply chain. The main quality attributes addressed by different schemes are the following:

- Farmers: the main quality attributes of the different schemes at farm level are the specific breeds, animal nutrition (natural products, safety), and extensive breeding methods.
- Industry (including slaughterhouses): the principal quality characteristics are animal welfare (transport and slaughtering) and hygienic conditions (fulfillment of UE rules).
- Retailers or butchers: the main characteristics are hygienic conditions of selling and availability of information related to traceability and origin.
- Public institutions (EU, national, regional): The main supported quality attributes are traceability, origin, safety in order to allow a product differentiation and an increase of consumers' confidence.

The only national scheme–the C.L.A.R.A. program–only gives guarantee that the beef and veal sold within the program are produced without using growth stimulators. This characteristic of meat is the most important safety concern for the consumers according to the results of our survey. Not a single case of BSE has been found in Spain, but quite often there are public accusations of illegal hormone practices.

A consumer organization (OCU) complains about the fact that the administration should guarantee to the consumers that all the beef and veal is sold in the market in this way, as the use of growth stimulators is illegal.

HOW DO POLICIES ADDRESS CONSUMER CONCERNS?

In general, CAP activities are focussed on the production side. However, quality programs are usually addressed to solve the problems of farmers, the marketing sector and the consumers. "Regional" quality programs (DPO, etc.), besides the protection of regional farmers and marketing agents, try to increase the consumer's security in health and nutritional values.

Sometimes, the consumer's concerns are not taken directly into consideration by the quality programs, but retailers, butchers or the civil servants represent their interests through marketing strategies. A consequence of these policies is the increase of quality control and market transparency. Consumers now have the possibility to buy certain regional products that are well-known due to their quality characteristics.

A significant amount of information to the consumer is transmitted by food labels, advertising and promotion. Label regulations may establish parameters for advertising, creating and limiting the franchise to advertise. In order to increase meat market transparency, symbols and labels are getting to be more and more important instruments. However, sometimes an excess of information may confuse consumers, as they may not be able to judge adequately the quality/price relationship. In any case labels act as a public surveillance assurance.

The importance of symbols and labels in the different steps of the meat chain can be assessed in the following way:

- Farmers usually have no labels, as they work within integrated quality programs. However, some labels allow the traceability of live animals and meat.
- Transformation industry (including slaughterhouses): They play an important role, as they control traceability of the meat.
- Usually each program has its own label for each one of the farmers and industries which cooperates within the quality program.
- Symbols and labels are especially important at the places of purchase. Retailers or butchers may sell meat proceeding of a national program or from their own quality one.
- Public institutions (EU, national, regional) give the legal requirements for using labels and symbols in order to avoid their fraudulent use.

RELATIONSHIPS BETWEEN AGRICULTURAL POLICY, QUALITY POLICY AND CONSUMER BEHAVIOR

Here we have a very general framework that may accomplish the whole horizon of the food chain, from the CAP in a macroeconomic view, to the quality policy ending in the consumer behavior. It is a great duel to analyze the interconnection, out of the goal of this paper, but it may give us some useful thoughts (Table 2), where we may get some relevant relationships among agricultural policy, quality policy and consumer behavior. Each one of the mentioned activities has several objectives (set of goals), desires some meat attributes and suggests different kinds of measures to achieve the goals.

Some factors (decrease of producer prices, deterioration of confidence in meat quality as perceived by consumers, etc.) try to modify quality policy in order to increase consumer confidence in meat quality.

However, some others tend to hinder a further increase of concerns of EU consumers regarding meat quality, as for example:

- Countries such as United States, Canada and Australia are in favor of trade liberalization in the meat market as a way to increase their exports to the EU. They do not accept the prohibition in the EU of selling meat produced with the utilization of growth stimulators, usual practice in their countries.

- Some Spanish entrepreneurs defend the use of artificial growers in beef and veal production as a way to assure the international competitiveness of the domestic producers. However, simultaneously they would like to participate in quality programs, which is not accepted by the actual regulation.
- Actual carcass standards enhance configuration and color of meat produced with growth stimulators so it is shown as more attractive to consumers. Therefore, there is a strong economic incentive for their use, especially in countries where the final fattening of the cattle should offset the scarcity of good grassland.
- Many consumers are not willing to pay higher prices for "high quality" meat and usually choose the cheaper one.
- It is interesting to mention that the UK government is in favor of decreasing meat prices at the EU market in order to diminish the surplus production, which is not accepted by many producers. On the other hand, many British consumers demand higher quality meat, with good sanitary control, so it will avoid the risks of BSE.

TABLE 2. Relationships Between Agricultural Policy, Quality Policy and Consumer Behavior

	Agricultural policy of the EU	Quality policy	Consumer behavior
Set of goals	– Increase of farmers' incomes and productivity, food security, market stability, adequate consumer prices, regional development, etc.	– Improvement of observed quality – Improvement of eating quality – Improvement of meat safety	– Improve observed quality – Improve eating quality – Improve meat safety
Set of attributes	– Sensorial – Security attributes – Nutritive – Economic – Social attributes, etc.	– Sensorial – Security attributes – Nutritive – Economic – Social attributes' etc.	– Most helpful attributes to assess: (a) meat quality in shops (beef): color and place of purchase; (b) Eating quality (beef: taste, tenderness and juiciness; (c) Meat safety (beef): growth stimulators.
Set of measures	– Measures with direct influence on the agricultural markets – Measures with indirect influences on the agricultural markets	– Product standards – Process standards – Consumer-oriented quality measures	– Measures with direct influence on agricultural markets – Measures with indirect influences on agricultural markets

SOURCE: Briz et al. 1998

CONSUMER BEHAVIOR

It is useful to analyze market evolution in recent years. During 1985-1994, Spanish consumers' expenditures in meat and meat products decreased from 8.3% to 6.1%. Chicken is the most consumed fresh meat followed by pork, beef and veal. It is quite useful to observe the substitution effect in the meat market. Thus, pork was the more important substitute product when the fish market had short supply. Since 1996, with the BSE and hormones affairs, pork has played a similar substitution role with beef and veal. Other types of meat like sheep, goat, rabbits and edible offal have more importance in Spain than in other European countries due to the consumption habits. On the opposite side, the consumption of frozen meat is remarkably low.

In a comparative analysis in 1995, the more expensive meats were, in annual average price, in preference order: veal, mutton, lamb and goat meat. The prices of beef and meat products were around average, while pork was below average. Poultry had the lowest prices. For similar kinds of meat, average prices paid by rich people were higher than the ones paid by lower income people due to the fact that they usually buy more noble pieces in more expensive retail shops. Prices were higher than average in traditional shops and lower in supermarkets and hypermarkets, where sale promotions are quite frequent.

Survey Results

According with the methodology mentioned, the inquiries analyzed the importance of several attributes for the different types of meat. In consumers' attitudes and behavior, we distinguish between the eating quality and meat quality in the shop. Flavor, tenderness and juiciness are important characteristics of the eating quality of beef and veal. Color and smell are considered in secondary range. In the case of pork, significant attributes are smell, flavor, tenderness, juiciness, color and texture. Similar to it is chicken, with the exception of texture. Leanness, and especially free of gristle are less important characteristics in the three types of meat. Regarding quality of meat at the selling place, characteristics observed may change while cooking or during the consumption. In the case of beef, veal, chicken and pork, consumer preferences are similar. The ranking of characteristics is the following: color is the main one, then leanness, brands, country of origin, and marbling. Price is considered the less important attribute.

It may be noted that the brand in no case is considered a significant factor for assessing the quality of meat at the shop. These results are somewhat surprising, considering the efforts of the administration and private enterprises to introduce brands in the meat market. To some extent, they can be explained by the fact that meat traditionally has been sold without any label or brand.

When we analyze consumers' concerns, the main factor in beef is the hormone content, while BSE is not as important as should be expected. This may be explained with the fact that there have been some cases of people intoxicated with the residues of growth enhancers in the last years and no one with BSE. It may be noted that the use of hormones is prohibited in Spain as in other EU countries. Nevertheless, there is a clandestine market to provide those products. Some mass media report very extensively each time that veterinarians find meat treated with those substances. This type of meat is usually sold in the national markets, and this may be the reason why the EU institutions cannot find these substances in traded meat. Concerning pork consumption, salmonella and hormones are declared problems, although there has been scarce information about the presence of hormones in pork. Small groups of people are concerned about fat/cholesterol in pork. In chicken, the pattern of concerns is rather similar to pork. The main characteristics for assessing the beef, pork and chicken safety are freshness and feed, more than country of origin, label or price. According to the consumer survey, about two-thirds of the respondents eat chicken at least twice a week. On the other hand, only one-third of the respondents eat pork, while beef and veal have an intermediate position. It should be noted that many people do not consume pork (24%) or beef (17%), while almost all the people asked consume chicken.

The main purchase place for all types of meat, and especially for beef and veal, is the butcher's shop, followed by the supermarket and local markets. However, in the period 1990-1995, the market share of butchers and other traditional shops in meat decreased from 60% to 43%. Meanwhile, the share of supermarkets increased from 27% to 34%, and the share of hypermarkets from 4% to 13%.

Attitude of Spanish Consumers

The attitude of the Spanish consumers towards meat is misleading. The majority of them consider that meat cannot be substituted easily and it is the base of good nutrition.

On the opposite side, others consider that the consumption of great quantities of meat and its products is not good for health. Consumers react promptly to the information published in the mass media in relation to factors like residue and naturalness. Recently the publications about the bovine spongiform encephalopathy in British cows–some specialists recommended the population not to consume beef and veal from Britain–caused a drop of the Spanish beef and veal prices by approximately 10%. This was the biggest in the last 30 years. After this price drop, some retailers put notes like "don't worry: we only sell beef and veal produced in controlled Spanish breeds and marketed with official origin or quality seals" in the entrance of their stores, until the market situation stabilized. A department of the Spanish Ministry of Agriculture gives these seals. Their importance has been growing in the last years because of the official quality policy–including advertising campaigns in television and other media–the social alarm about hormone residues found in meat, and other factors.

Among the main factors, which influence the consumers' decisions, we found price, quality, tenderness and taste. However, there is an increase importance of other characteristics: income, health (fat-pig meat), environment, fears about growth enhancers (beef and veal), salmonellas (poultry meat), and cholesterol (red meat).

We may observe a price segmentation of the meat market, as many consumers are willing to pay higher prices for better products with a guaranteed quality. Thus, the market share of veal, poultry, and other meat products, marketed with generic (official) quality seals like designations of origin, ecological product, etc., is increasing. At the same time, brands of meat industries, retailers and restaurant chains that guarantee the meat quality (free from hormones, ecological, etc.) are growing in importance.

According to our survey, most of the respondents strongly agree (55%) or just agree (23%) when being asked if they are able to assess properly the eating quality of meat in the shop just by looking at it. More than half of the respondents (55%) like it a lot to taste new recipes, and 16% simply like to try them. Almost half of the respondents (45%) do not like cooking, but consider it a necessary activity. However, other respondents (35%) like cooking and do not believe that it is just a necessary task. Many people (80%) completely agree to the statement that "we should have more respect for animals." A majority of the respondents (75%) prefer to buy meat from well-treated animals. However, these high percentages are more theoretical than a real willingness to achieve a better animal welfare by paying higher prices for livestock with any "animal welfare label." In fact, the Administration did not put forth legal proposals for improving animal welfare in some production systems (e.g. poultry), considering the negative aspects on productivity and competitiveness with other imported products.

On another scenario, most of the consumers consider that food is healthy. Among the respondents there seems to be a high preference for buying food locally produced (75% completely agree). However, in many cases, this is not possible due to the lower competitiveness in relation to other products. The great majority of respondents like to know from which country the meat comes. For that reason, for beef and veal quite frequently the regional origin is indicated, even in the meat without the label of Denomination of Origin. Spain nearly has a trade balance in equilibrium with beef and veal. Although there is some trade with fresh and frozen beef and veal, consumers usually eat national products. Unlike in other EU countries, such as Sweden, there is no label indicating the Spanish origin of the meat, but there are several seals indicating the regional origin within Spain (e.g., "Ternera Gallega," "Carne de Avila," etc.). The meat imported from some countries, as for instance Argentina and Uruguay, also has a good image among consumers.

In general, consumers believe that meat is essential for a balanced diet. In Spain, only a few people do not eat meat at all. More than half of the respondents think that there are other sources of protein besides meat, supposedly fish, although it is not directly mentioned. Traditionally, fresh meat usually has been sold without any label or brand in Spain, while there have been some brands in the meat-products market. The decreasing demand of beef and veal gives more relevance to labels in this market (Denominations of Origin, Clara program, etc.). There is one D.O. in the chicken market. Some enterprises in the chicken and meat processing industry have gotten the ISO certification. Nowadays fresh meat sold under official quality labels is only 5% of the total amount in Spain. However, meat sold under retailers' quality labels have a higher percentage. The fact that most of the hypermarkets and supermarkets are introducing retailer brands indicates that consumers react positively in some way to this marketing strategy. So, proliferation of many quality brands may be confusing to some consumers. In the sample, when respondents looked at the labels about meat safety, they trusted more origin labels and quality symbols of beef and veal, origin labels and health stamps of pork, and slaughtering house stamps and origin labels in the case of chicken.

Table 3 shows the absolute frequencies of the answers related to the trust on the information sources about meat safety. When looking for information

TABLE 3. Trust on Information Sources About Meat Safety

	Beef	Pork	Chicken
Government	10	16	8
Ministry of Agriculture	8	7	5
Minist. of Health & Consumption	35	18	14
Consumers associations	26	18	12
Independent butchers	183	71	52
Butchers at supermarkets	85	51	45
Friends	9	8	–
Magazines	9	5	–
Reports	6	13	–
Radio reports	–	6	–
Health bureau	6	7	–
Mother, other family persons	14	7	–
I trust myself	35	12	–
None/don't know	54	197	90

Source: EU.FAIR CT 950046–Survey in Spanish Market

on meat safety, people trust more independent butchers than supermarkets. Concerning this matter, when judging information provided by institutions, respondents also have confidence in the Ministry of Health and Consumption and consumer organizations.

CONCLUSIONS

The article may be considered as an attention call about the necessity to look for a more coordinated action among different segments of the meat sector. Quite often, we find excellent researchers with a very narrow scope. However, the interaction among the different pieces of the puzzle in most of the agribusiness sectors is made necessary to establish the adequate relationship in order to know the causes and the effects, and the consumer reactions to some quality policies. In comparison to other EU member states (Sweden, United Kingdom and Germany), the Spanish situation shows a lower degree of analysis of consumer behavior. Some other aspects such as concerns for animal welfare are not significant in Spain.

A large share of the respondents consume meat twice or more a week. Most people think that meat is an essential part of the meal. The main place of purchase of fresh meat is the butcher, but super and hypermarkets are increasing their market shares.

The flavor, the tenderness, and the juiciness are considered to be the most important characteristics of beef and veal, while in the case of pork and chicken, there are a wide range of characteristics which are important. When assessing the quality of meat in the shop, the color and the place of purchase are considered as the most important factors. Most respondents think that they are able to assess quality of meat in the shop just by looking at it.

About safety concerns, most people are concerned about hormones (beef and veal); salmonella, hormones and antibiotics (pork); and salmonella and hormones (chicken). It becomes clear that they do not trust the institutions that are responsible for controlling the carrying out of the laws that prohibit the use of hormones. However, most respondents believe that the foods that they buy in the shops are safe.

Most people declare that they care a lot about animal welfare. However, the willingness to pay higher prices for meat from well treated animals is limited, but they are in favor of paying a higher price to get a good piece of meat. Indeed, people with high income usually eat less meat than people with low income but they pay higher prices per kilo of each type of meat. Most respondents prefer food produced locally, but in many regions local production is lower than the consumption. Therefore, most food has to be imported from other regions. Many consumers prefer to know the origin (country, region) of the meat they buy; however, until recently retailers usually sold fresh meat without any quality label or identification, although there were some health standards that had to be fulfilled.

In the last years, quality seals, Denomination of Origin, and brands have gotten increasingly important. In this way, the study tried to achieve market segmentation and to increase the trust of the consumers on acquiring meat of good quality. When looking for information on the safety of meat, people trust most independent butchers than butchers in the supermarkets. Among the institutions, respondents trust more the Ministry of Health and Consumption concerning meat safety.

The quality safety of meat products should take into consideration the confidence of many consumers in the butchers. The implementation of quality seals and brands in the fresh meat market seems to be useful. However, it should be made sure that consumers know enough about the meaning of each label. Only thus, will these labels really become useful information and increase the trust of the consumers in the quality of the meat that they buy.

There seems to be a need to improve the trust of the consumers in public institutions when they look for information on the safety of meat. Nowadays, only the Ministry of Health and Consumption has acceptable results about this question. It might be useful to work with consumer associations when implementing the quality policy concerning meat.

If the quality policy measures that have been introduced recently are implemented in a serious way, and they are complemented with the measures mentioned above, an increase of the consumer's trust in the meat quality, and as a consequence stabilization or even increase of the meat demand, seems feasible.

The negative price trends in the beef, veal and pork markets made necessary the implementation of quality programs. These programs assure, for the first time, the traceability of the beef, veal and pork sold in the stores. Most of them are having a satisfactory acceptance among consumers, but their market share is still very low. It is very important to maintain and increase the consumer's confidence in fresh meat, so programs will give more reliability to consumers. Otherwise, the image of these programs could be seriously damaged.

The survey shows some of the characteristics that are considered more important by consumers concerning meat safety, quality in the shop, eating quality, etc.

In order to get back the confidence of the consumers, according to the results of the survey, it should be positive to involve the traditional retailers and consumer's associations in quality policies. In some hypermarkets, changes have taken place changes in this sense.

The future will show if the importance of quality policies will continue increasing and the programs will get a similar market share as in other

European countries. Quality programs should rely progressing on marketing mix strategies. In the coming future, the meat market will be more competitive with the liberalization of foreign trade. In consequence, consumer behavior will be more oriented by an increasing role of private enterprises in a globalization process. Traditional consumers will overlap with modern consumption habits and competition will define the market border lines.

REFERENCES

Alvensleben, R. (1997) *Agrofood Marketing* Ed. Padberg et al. CAB. International CIHEAM. N. York.

Becker, T., Glitsch, K., Benner, E., (1996) *Quality Policy and Consumer Behavior.* *Annual Program Report.* EU FAIR-CT 95-0046. DG 12-SSMA.

Briz, J., Mahlau, M., Gutierrez, E. (1997) *Report on Consumer Perception of Meat Quality in Spain.* EU FAIR-CT 95-46. Madrid (Spain).

Briz, J., Mahlau, M., Gutierrez, E. (1998) *Links Between Quality Policy and Consumer Behavior in Spain.* EU FAIR–CT 95-0046. Madrid (Spain).

Furitsch, H.P. (1994) *Social Welfare Development and Food Demand: Foundation and Empirical Analysis in the Case of the Demand for Food and Meat in Spain.* (German Version). Europäische Hochschulschriften. BD: 1540 Frankfurt.

Grunert, K. et al. (1993) *Food-related lifestyle: Development of a Cross Culturally Valid Instrument for Market Surveillance.* MAPP working paper num. 12. Aarhus Denmark.

Grunert, K. et al. (1996) *Market Orientation in Food and Agriculture.* Kluwer Academic Publ. MA.

Instituto Nacional de Estadística (1994) *Encuesta de Presupuestos Familiares 1990-91,* Madrid.

Nielsen, N.A., (1998) *The Beef Market in the European Union.* Working Paper num. 51. January. MAPP. Denmark.

Senauer, B. et al. (1991) *Food Trends and the Changing Consumer.* Eagan Press. St Paul MN.

Splitters, P. (1993) *Image and Meat Consumption, Meat Consumption in the European Communities,* European Commission, Brussels.

Current Status and Competitiveness of U.S. Poultry Exports

Kristin Michel
Conrado M. Gempesaw II
Courtney S. Biery

SUMMARY. The general objective of this study is to analyze the comparative advantage and future prospects of the U.S. poultry industry in the international arena. The domestic resource cost (DRC) ratio was estimated for the five largest poultry exporters in the world. The DRC ratio provides a comparison of economic advantages/disadvantages in poultry trade. In addition, an analysis of the future of international poultry trade was conducted based on published forecasts.

Published studies have shown that poultry production and consumption are expected to increase in most countries. The United States, having one of the better DRC ratios, is predicted to retain its majority position in international poultry trade as export growth slows in the European Union and Thailand. However, domestic production in Hong Kong/China will pose a threat to U.S. exports along with the expected growth in the Brazilian poultry industry. *[Article copies available for a fee from The Haworth Document Delivery Service: 1-800-342-9678. E-mail address: getinfo@haworthpressinc.com <Website: http://www.haworthpressinc.com>]*

Kristin Michel is a former Graduate Research Assistant, Conrado M. Gempesaw II is Professor and Chair, and Courtney S. Biery is a Undergraduate Research Assistant, all affiliated with Delaware Agricultural Experiment Station, Department of Food and Resource Economics, College of Agriculture and Natural Resources, University of Delaware, Newark, DE, 19717-1303.

Published as Paper No. 1652 in the Journal Series of the Delaware Agricultural Experiment Station.

[Haworth co-indexing entry note]: "Current Status and Competitiveness of U.S. Poultry Exports." Michel, Kristen, Conrado M. Gempesaw II, and Courtney S. Biery. Co-published simultaneously in *Journal of International Food & Agribusiness Marketing* (International Business Press, an imprint of The Haworth Press, Inc.) Vol. 10, No. 4, 1999, pp. 63-76; and: *Cross-National and Cross-Cultural Issues in Food Marketing* (ed: Erdener Kaynak) International Business Press, an imprint of The Haworth Press, Inc., 1999, pp. 63-76. Single or multiple copies of this article are available for a fee from The Haworth Document Delivery Service [1-800-342-9678, 9:00 a.m. - 5:00 p.m. (EST). E-mail address: getinfo@haworthpressinc.com].

KEYWORDS. U.S. poultry exports, competitiveness, the domestic resource cost, European Union, East Asian countries

INTRODUCTION

With the help of economic liberalization in China and Russia along with the growing incomes in developing nations, the United States poultry industry is currently thriving. In the past, the poultry industry expanded mostly through increases in consumption by U.S. consumers. Between 1990 and 1997, however, domestic consumption only grew annually by roughly 3 percent, but international consumption grew at much higher levels, especially in certain developing countries in Asia (USA Poultry & Egg Export Council, 1996 and Henry and Rothwell, 1995). The United States is the largest poultry exporter in the world, with international export volume of 43 percent in 1997 (USDA, FAS, October 1997). This competitive position is achieved through highly developed technology and relatively low costs of production. But where will the U.S. poultry industry stand in the international market in the future? The general objective of this study is to analyze the comparative advantage and future prospects of the U.S. poultry industry in the international arena.

THE POULTRY INDUSTRY IN THE UNITED STATES

The United States currently leads the world in both poultry exports and production (Figures 1 and 2). Access to feed grains and technological efficiencies make the U.S. a low cost producer. The domestic consumption rate, at 47 kg per capita, is one of the highest in the world but consumption rates are growing faster in some other countries (USA Poultry & Egg Export Council, 1996). Between 1988 and 1993, U.S. poultry consumption increased 5.1 percent per year, while for the same time period in Hong Kong and China, consumption increased 11.4 percent and 13.4 percent per year, respectively. Per capita consumption figures are given for selected countries in Figure 3 (Henry and Rothwell, 1995).

Over the last forty years, the U.S. poultry industry has experienced huge production gains. Production data for major producers are presented in Figure 2 for selected years from 1975 through 1998. In some years the positive change in production has been as high as 27 percent (USA Poultry & Egg Export Council, 1996). During the period of 1980 to 1993, poultry production increased by 88 percent (Roenigk, 1993). It is forecasted that production in 1998 will reach 15.9 million metric tons up from 15 million metric tons in 1997 (USDA, FAS, October 1997).

FIGURE 1. Poultry Exporting Countries and Amounts

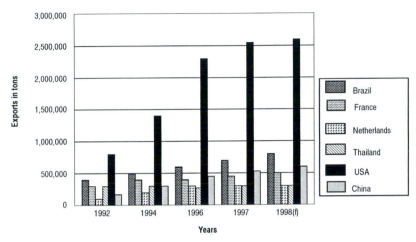

Sources: Henry and Rothwell, 1995 and *Livestock and Poultry: World Markets and Trade,* USDA, FAS

Exports grew slowly and then rapidly over the last two decades. In 1980, the U.S. exported 5 percent of production and by 1990, 6 percent of production. By 1995, however, exports reached 15.7 percent of production. In 1996, the USA Poultry & Egg Export Council predicted that more than 20 percent of U.S. poultry production would be exported by the year 2000. The 1997 export amount was 2.5 million metric tons accounting for 17 percent of total poultry production in the U.S. (USDA, FAS, October 1997). The primary markets for U.S. poultry exports are Russia and Hong Kong/China. Other export markets are Japan, Mexico, Canada, and the Middle East (Henry and Rothwell, 1995).

EXPORTING NATIONS

International poultry trade is growing. The principal poultry exporting countries are Brazil, France, the Netherlands, Thailand, and the United States. Selected countries and their export amounts are shown in Figure 1 for 1992, 1994, 1996, 1997, and 1998 (forecasted). In 1988, 6.3 percent of world production was traded internationally (this includes intra-European Union trade). Ten years later in 1997, 11 percent of world production was traded internationally, approximately 5.9 million tons of poultry. In 1998, poultry trade is expected to increase to 6.3 million tons, up 6 percent from 1997 (USDA, FAS, October 1997).

During the 1980s and early 1990s poultry production in Brazil increased annually at rates of approximately 10 percent (Figure 2). The industry was able to grow at such high rates because of low costs, growing domestic consumption, and a competitively priced product in the world market (Henry and Rothwell, 1995). In 1998, production is forecasted to be 4.7 million metric tons of ready to cook poultry meat (USDA, FAS, October 1997).

In the international market, Brazil has been increasing exports at an average rate of over 12 percent annually since 1987. Brazilian exports are expected to reach 740,000 metric tons next year (Figure 1). Fifteen percent of Brazil's total broiler production in 1997 (670,000 tons) were exported (USDA, FAS, October 1997).

France and the Netherlands are the major poultry producers and exporters in the European Union. Forecasted 1998 production in France is 2.3 million metric tons, while for the Netherlands it is almost 730,000 metric tons of ready to cook equivalents (Figure 2). European demand is expected to remain strong although not growing in the same way as it did in 1996 and 1997. Costs of production, however, are high on a relative international basis due to high feed costs, high labor costs, and stringent environmental restrictions. In the past, Europe has used subsidies for exports of poultry in an attempt to overcome these disadvantages and make its poultry competitive in the international market. With the signing of the last GATT agreement, subsidized exports are being decreased each year. In an environment of growing world demand, European producers are having to adjust to these new policies but

FIGURE 2. International Poultry Production

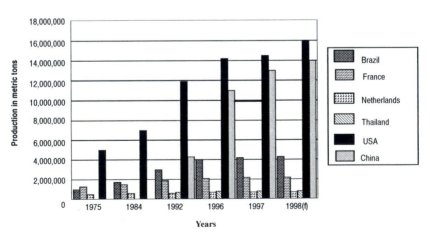

Sources: *World Indices of Agricultural and Food Production, 1975-1984*, ERS, 1985 and *Livestock and Poultry: World Markets and Trade*, USDA, FAS, October 1996 and 1997.
(f) forecast

FIGURE 3. Per Capita Poultry Meat Consumption

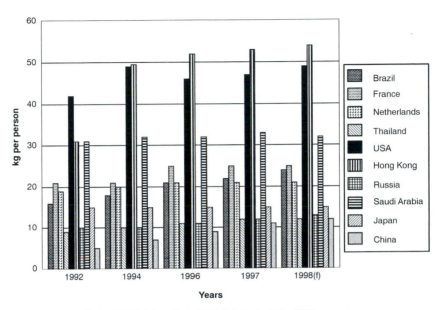

Sources: *Livestock and Poultry: World Markets and Trade*, USDA, FAS, October 1996 and 1997.
(f) forecast

are still expected to increase their exports each year (USDA, FAS, October 1996 and 1997).

The poultry industry in Thailand grew at an annual rate of approximately 8 percent during the 1980s. Much of this growth was due to low labor and feed costs which made Thailand's poultry producers competitive in the world market. Recently the competitive position of Thailand has been eroded by increased competition in the form of lower labor costs in China and also by domestic problems of labor shortages, higher feed costs due to currency devaluation, and a limited amount of land for poultry production. Domestic demand continues to be strong, however, as incomes rise and tastes change. In 1998, a 5 percent increase in production is expected to over one million metric tons (Figure 2). Thai exports suffered after China began exporting to Japan. However, due to its latest major currency devaluation, Thai exports will become more competitive in the Japanese market. In 1997, exports increased by almost 11 percent to 187,000 metric tons and a 7 percent rise is expected in 1998 (Henry and Rothwell, 1995 and USDA, FAS, October 1997).

China, one of the fastest growing developing economies, has emerged in the past few years as the second largest poultry producer in the world. At the same time, the country is one of the larger poultry importing markets. Due to rising incomes, a large and growing population, and changing tastes, poultry consumption in China is expected to show strong growth for many years to come. Production in China in 1998 is projected to be 14 million metric tons, a 12 percent increase from 1997. Of this production, approximately 650,000 metric tons are forecasted to be exported (USDA, FAS, October 1997).

IMPORTING NATIONS

The major poultry importing countries and regions of the world are the former Soviet Union led by Russia, Hong Kong/China, Japan, and the Middle East led by Saudi Arabia. Figure 4 contains information on imports for these countries from 1988 to 1998 (forecasted). The Russian and Chinese markets account for approximately 65 percent of world imports. As these countries' imports decrease, gains in poultry meat trade will slow. Chinese prices have begun to fall as a result of domestic production gains (USDA, FAS, October 1997). Major exporters will find it hard to compete with China's domestic poultry prices. Over the next 9 years, the USDA expects imports to increase by 6.75 percent annually in China and 3 percent annually in Hong Kong. In 1997, however, Chinese and Hong Kong imports increased 20 and 15 percent, respectively, from 1996 (Figure 4).

FIGURE 4. Poultry Importing Countries

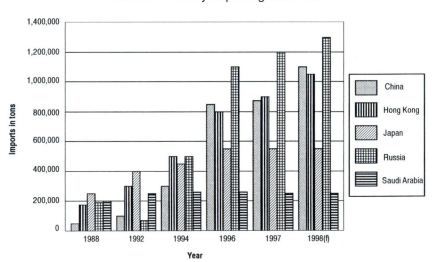

Sources: Henry and Rothwell, 1995 and *Livestock and Poultry: World Markets and Trade*, USDA, FAS, October 1996 and 1997.

After a 60 percent decline due to high production costs, poultry production in Russia will bottom out this year. Stabilization in the Russian market will affect exports to Russia. The USDA forecasts an increase of less than one percent for Russian imports over the next nine years.

The USDA predicts a decrease in Saudi Arabian imports between 1997 and 2005 (Figure 4). In an attempt to become more self-sufficient, Saudi Arabia has targeted the poultry production sector. Production increased 29 percent in 1997 over 1996 levels. By 2005, imports to Saudi Arabia will grow by only one percent.

Imports into Korea, Romania and Mexico continue to look favorable due to improved government policies. The Korean poultry quota was replaced by a tariff allowing for less complicated trade. The Romanian government implemented a new set of import duties, lowering tariffs by 60 percent. Higher pork prices in Mexico prompted the Mexican government to increase the maximum limits on turkey imports (USDA, FAS, October 1997).

Japan is also a large market for poultry. The annual per capita rate of consumption was 14.3 kg in 1997. Due to the large number of people on the small island and the limited space for livestock production, Japan is a prime export market for poultry and other meats. Also, because of the high price commanded in this market, it is a desirable destination for most poultry exporting nations (Henry and Rothwell, 1995).

DOMESTIC RESOURCE COSTS IN THE INTERNATIONAL POULTRY INDUSTRY

While the United States poultry industry is the world's leading exporter, other countries may also have economic advantages for poultry exports. A method called the Domestic Resource Cost (DRC) ratio can be used to investigate efficiencies and comparative advantages among the poultry exporting nations. This method compares the cost to produce a commodity domestically with the price received for the commodity in the world market. If the ratio is equal to one, the cost to produce it domestically and buy it internationally are the same and there is no comparative advantage or disadvantage. If the ratio is less than one, the cost to produce the good domestically is less than the cost to buy it on the world market and a comparative advantage exists. Conversely, if the ratio is greater than one, the cost of producing the good domestically is greater than the price to buy it on the world market and a comparative disadvantage exists.

The DRC procedure in this study follows from the research done by Michel (1997). The cost of production data used in the ratio are denominated in US$/kg produced. To keep the rest of the study consistent, all other data were converted to this unit following the Michel study. The DRC equation used in this study can be specified as follows:

$$DRC = \frac{N_j}{P_{kj} - T_j}$$

where

N_j = the domestic non-tradable input dollar cost per kilogram produced in country j,

P_{kj} = the dollar price received for the product by export country j in import country k, and

T_j = the tradable dollar input cost in export country j.

In poultry production, the main tradable input is feed. For the sake of simplicity in this study, feed cost was used as the tradable input for production and all other input factors were considered domestic non-tradable costs. Poultry input costs are generally thought to have little distortion from true market prices. Because of this, shadow prices were set equal to market prices for inputs. There are, however, instances where distortions affect poultry input and output prices, such as in the European Union where feed grain prices are elevated due to agricultural policies. European producers are generally compensated with export subsidies. The European Union seems to be the market where the most distortions occur on a relative basis but even compared to other agricultural products, the poultry market distortions in Europe are relatively small. Therefore, market prices were used for tradable and non-tradable inputs in this study and in the case of Europe, where price distortions may be occurring, the distortions were accounted for, if possible. The prices received for poultry in import markets covers all shadow costs such as transportation, insurance, storage, and distribution.

The principal exporting nations are compared in this study to determine which countries have the greatest advantages in the world market. The results are presented in Table 1 and are based on 1994 cost of production and price data. Because the price of a good is often different in various markets due to transportation costs and other factors, the results are categorized by exporting country and importing market.

In general, the countries with the lowest costs of production tend to have the best comparative advantages as indicated by the DRC ratio. Brazil is the lowest cost producer in the world. The United States and Thailand follow in second and third place, while France and the Netherlands exhibit the highest costs of production (Henry and Rothwell, 1995). Brazil, with its low costs,

TABLE 1. Results of the Domestic Resource Cost Ratio

Import Country	Export Country	DRC Ratio	Amount (metric tons)
Hong Kong	Brazil	0.760	40,599
	France	1.729	11,368
	Netherlands	1.632	25,421
	Thailand	1.637	7,366
	United States	1.114	327,216
Japan	Brazil	0.291	152,403
	France	0.353	2,568
	Thailand	0.226	134,017
	United States	0.470	223,450
Jordan	Thailand	0.318	616
	France	2.609	5,117
Kuwait	Brazil	0.539	18,328
	France	1.603	9,742
	United States	0.440	2,089
Middle East	Brazil	0.438	N/A
	France	1.105	N/A
	Netherlands	1.154	N/A
	Thailand	0.564	N/A
	United States	0.608	N/A
Oman	Brazil	0.663	1,420
	France	1.948	997
	Netherlands	1.680	471
	United States	0.889	3,049
Russia	France	0.868	4,874
	Netherlands	1.507	31,825
	United States	0.636	146,155

Sources: *The World Poultry Industry,* Henry and Rothwell, 1995, "1994 UN Commodity Trade
Statistics," 1995, and FAS of the USDA 1995 unpublished data.
N/A: Not Available. The Middle East in this table is comprised of Egypt, Jordan, Kuwait, and Oman. The total amount of poultry imported
by these countries is 85,961 metric tons.

has a comparative advantage in every market into which it exports. France
and the Netherlands, with their costs of production, show a comparative
disadvantage in a majority of the markets. One of the exceptions is Japan
where poultry is sold at higher prices than it is sold in the rest of the world.
High prices in the import market compensate for high prices in the production market and tend to give every country a comparative advantage, as in the
case of Japan.

The United States DRC ratios show comparative advantages in all markets
except Hong Kong. A good deal of what is exported to Hong Kong is
re-exported to China so this market includes both countries. It is interesting to
note that while the U.S. is by far the largest exporter to Hong Kong/China, it
exports at a comparative disadvantage. An explanation for this may lie in the
type of poultry demanded in that market. Much of what is exported to Hong
Kong/China is dark meat and chicken feet, products that do not command a high
price in the United States. In fact, Chinese consumers tend to have a preference
for gizzards, feet, chicken heads, and necks, all parts which are not widely

consumed in the U.S. (USDA, FAS, October 1996). Consumers in the U.S. demand white meat and pay a higher price for it. In 1994, the average retail price paid in the U.S. for chicken breast with the bone in was 454.37 cents per kilogram. At the same time, the average cost of production was 105.0 cents per kilogram (USDA, ERS, 1997 and Henry and Rothwell, 1995). The higher priced white meat could very well be supporting the production process and allowing U.S. producers to export other chicken parts at lower costs. A comparative disadvantage may not, in fact, be present in this case. Rather, low cost poultry parts supported by the sale of higher priced parts in the domestic market may simply be dominating the market because of very competitive costs.

Another important market for the United States is Russia. In this market, the U.S. has a definite comparative advantage and also exports the largest amount of poultry. Again, the type of poultry that the U.S. exports to Russia is mostly dark meat in the form of chicken legs. These chicken legs are popular both because of price and quality. Sausages are also popular in Russia and to capitalize on this market, U.S. poultry companies have begun to export chicken franks (USDA, FAS, *Annual Marketing Plan,* Russia, 1996). Russian demand for U.S. poultry has increased to the point that as of 1996, Russia imported approximately 40 percent of all U.S. poultry exports and was the largest market for U.S. poultry exports (USDA, FAS, October 1996).

THE FUTURE OF INTERNATIONAL POULTRY TRADE

The United States Department of Agriculture (USDA) looked at the future of international poultry trade to year 2005 (USDA, 1997). The Organization for Economic Co-operation and Development (OECD) projected production figures and prices for the world poultry market (OECD, 1997). Both forecasts anticipate slower growth in poultry production than in the past. However, consumption will continue to increase as demand for all meat products increase with changes in meat demand and rising incomes (USDA, FAS, October 1997).

The United States is expected to increase exports by between 4 and 5 percent annually through 2005 and to continue to be the largest poultry exporter in the world. The U.S., however, will experience increasing pressure from competitor products causing the demand for broiler meat exports to slow. A more optimistic forecast is provided by the OECD which predicts an annual growth rate of 7.5 percent in U.S. exports during the next five years. Brazil is also expected to increase exports and is expected to be the second largest exporter by 2005. With an annual growth rate over the next five years of −4.52 percent, the European Union's exports will decrease. The USDA predicts that the EU will fall behind Brazil's exports to become the third largest poultry exporter in the world.

Lower prices and convenience of processed poultry products have caused people in China, Mexico, and Russia to consume more poultry. China has responded by expanding its domestic poultry meat production. The Asian and Russian financial crises have also increased competition among global meat producers. Domestic poultry prices in importing nations are becoming more competitive than imported poultry prices limiting the demand for U.S. imports (USDA, ERS, June-July 1998). Russia, an importer of 40-45 percent of U.S. exports in 1997, will probably import less poultry due to their economic crisis and currency devaluation. However, it is possible that increased consumption of poultry may outweigh the effects of the devaluation of the ruble. Poultry is the least expensive meat and therefore, the most demanded meat by Russian consumers. Domestic production in Russia will be incapable of meeting the demand for poultry and imports of U.S. poultry could be likely in spite of Russia's current economic troubles (USDA, ERS, October 1998).

The currency devaluation in Thailand will make Thai exports more attractive to Japan. Unfortunately, higher imported feed prices will prevent Thailand from increasing production of exports to Japan. Thailand's exports are expected to remain at the same levels or possibly fall in the future (USDA, FAS, October 1996 and 1997). The USDA predicts an annual growth rate of less than one percent for Thai exports during the next eight years (USDA, FAS, October 1997 and OECD).

Looking to the future, it can be surmised that poultry production, consumption, and trade are expected to increase internationally (Figures 2 and 3). This is good news for poultry producers, especially those with the best comparative advantages in production. The United States is predicted to retain its majority position in international poultry trade, perhaps capitalizing on growing markets in developing countries and expected lower growths of exports from the European Union and Thailand. However, as domestic production begins to increase, Hong Kong/China poses a threat to U.S. exports. Also, some of these optimistic projections may have to be revised downwards given the current economic problems in Asia and Russia. The other issue that has not been considered in these projections was the recent bird-flu problem affecting Hong Kong and Chinese poultry markets.

CONCLUSION

As the developing nations of the world gain in economic strength, the incomes of their citizens are rapidly increasing. Higher incomes allow people to vary their protein sources and, typically, the demand for poultry increases. For the U.S. poultry industry, this is a positive trend because greater demand in world markets means that the U.S. can supply more poultry to meet that demand.

Generally, poultry from the U.S. is sold in foreign markets at a comparative advantage. Where a comparative disadvantage exists, as in the case of Hong Kong, the strong demand for high priced white meat in the domestic U.S. market is supporting the low cost of dark meat and other poultry parts exported to foreign markets. This is an important benefit for U.S. poultry exporters because producers are able to price their product competitively and in such a way as to capture a large market share in many foreign countries.

The future of the international poultry industry is likely to change in several ways. One of the changes could include an increase in demand for poultry prepared products. Such a change is evidenced in the U.S. domestic market as "easy to prepare" products are gaining strength in supermarkets. Such a trend in the international poultry market will depend on the increased use of labor in the poultry processing stage. This will benefit countries with low costs of labor and could be a liability to countries with higher labor costs. The U.S. has relatively high labor costs compared to other poultry exporting countries. This could prove to be a weakness for U.S. poultry exports unless the demand for poultry parts with little value added processing remains strong.

One issue that could slow the growth of poultry imports into developing countries is the lack of general infrastructure in the way of seaports and roadways and, in particular, in the way of refrigeration facilities to store frozen poultry. Countries such as India, Malaysia, Vietnam, and China are all struggling with these issues in one way or another. The speed with which infrastructure is developed will have a great effect on the growth of poultry imports into these countries.

Another issue that will be important in the international poultry market in the future is the ease with which poultry production technology can be transferred between countries. Only a limited amount of land is necessary for raising poultry so even countries with a lack of space can produce a considerable amount of poultry. In this case, the demand for grain as feed for growing chickens should increase. Grain is easier to store and transport than frozen poultry. The U.S. grain industry will most likely benefit from such a situation but the U.S. poultry industry, insofar as it is increasingly dependent on international trade, may be affected by this easy transfer of poultry technology. In all reality, however, it must be remembered that in the past when poultry production technology was transferred out of the U.S. like it was to Europe in the 1960s, the growth in demand for poultry worldwide eventually outgrew the new production capability and the U.S. poultry industry benefited anyway. The market changed but overall demand for poultry grew. This could very well be what happens in world poultry market in the near future. The important thing for the U.S. poultry industry is to always be ready to enter the newest developing markets in the world.

A third factor that can affect the competitive advantage of the U.S. poultry industry is the rapid development of the Brazilian poultry industry. Currently, whole chickens sold in the Brazilian domestic market are bringing in close to zero profits. Brazilian producers are targeting new export markets such as South Africa, Cuba, and Russia. To obtain higher profit margins, Brazilian producers are exploring products with more value-added components such as breaded chicken pieces and cooked chicken joints. Cheap feed prices will help keep Brazilian poultry production strong and maintain their position as one of the largest poultry producers, second only to the U.S. (Paulo, 1998).

Finally, a critical issue that needs to be considered is the push towards free trade among nations. Poultry producing countries with comparative advantages are expected to benefit from trade liberalization. World poultry trade is expected to increase because the effects of free trade will cause domestic prices to fall. U.S. poultry exports should gain due to its comparative advantage in both poultry and feed grain production.

The future of the U.S. poultry industry looks strong both because of high levels of domestic demand and growing international demand as incomes rise in developing countries. Poultry from the U.S. is competitive in world markets and looks to remain so in the future. It will, however, be important for the industry to capture new markets to decrease dependency on a few markets and to cushion against importing countries that develop their own domestic poultry production.

REFERENCES

Henry, R., and G. Rothwell. 1995. *The World Poultry Industry.* Published by the World Bank and the International Finance Corporation, Washington, DC.

Michel, K. 1997. "A Modified Policy Delphi Approach to Projecting International Trade in Poultry." Unpublished Master's Thesis, University of Delaware, Department of Food and Resource Economics. Newark, DE.

OECD. 1997. *The Agricultural Outlook 1997-2001.* Organization for Economic Co-operation and Development. Paris, France.

Paulo, San. April, 1998. "All clucked up." *The Economist.* New York: The Economist Newspaper Limited.

Roenigk, W. 1993. "World Poultry Sector Continues Dramatic Expansion." *Smith-Kline Beecham Avian News.* Exton, PA.

USA Poultry & Egg Export Council. 1996. Statistical Data Sheets. Atlanta, GA.

USDA. 1997. *Agricultural Baseline Projections to 2005, Reflecting the 1996 Farm Act.* Interagency Agricultural Projections Committee. Staff Report WAOB-97-1. Washington, DC.

USDA, ERS. 1997. *Poultry Yearbook.* United States Department of Agriculture, Economic Research Service, Washington, D.C. Stock #89007B.

USDA, ERS. June-July, 1998. *Agricultural Outlook.* United States Department of Agriculture, Economic Research Service, Washington, D.C. Stock #AGO-252.

USDA, ERS. October, 1998. *Agricultural Outlook.* United States Department of Agriculture, Economic Research Service, Washington, D.C. Stock #AGO-255.

USDA, FAS. 1996. *Annual Marketing Plan.* United States Department of Agriculture, Foreign Agriculture Service. AGR Number RS6052. American Embassy, Moscow, Russia.

USDA, FAS. October, 1996. *Livestock and Poultry: World Markets and Trade, October 1996.* United States Department of Agriculture, Foreign Agricultural Service. Circular Series FL&P 2-96. Washington, D.C.

USDA, FAS. October, 1997. *Livestock and Poultry: World Markets and Trade, October 1997.* United States Department of Agriculture, Foreign Agricultural Service. Circular Series FL&P 2-97. Washington, D.C.

Pan-European Food Market Segmentation: An Application to the Yoghurt Market in the EU

Carlotta Valli
Rupert J. Loader
W. Bruce Traill

SUMMARY. An increasingly competitive international environment makes it necessary for firms to focus more and more on cross-country consumer segments. This increases the importance of international market segmentation and the need to develop new research approaches. The aim of this work is to present some of the results of a yoghurt segmentation study across Europe based on an innovative consumer measure explaining motivation to food choice, and to discuss the strategic implications of cross-country segments. The segmentation exercise identifies four pan-European segments with respect to yoghurt. The approach used for market segmentation proves to have important strategic implications, especially for the development of standardized product positioning concepts and communication strategy. *[Article copies available for a fee from*

Carlotta Valli is a Doctoral Student, Rupert J. Loader is Lecturer in Food Economics and Marketing, and W. Bruce Traill is Professor of Food Management and Marketing, all with the Department of Agricultural and Food Economics, The University of Reading, UK.

Address correspondence to: Carlotta Valli, Department of Agricultural and Food Economics, The University of Reading, 4 Earley Gate, Whiteknights Road, Reading RG6 6AR, UK. (E-mail: C.Valli@reading.ac.uk).

The authors would like to thank the Commission of the European Communities for research support (Project AIR2-CT94-1066).

[Haworth co-indexing entry note]: "Pan-European Food Market Segmentation: An Application to the Yoghurt Market in the EU." Valli, Carlotta, Rupert J. Loader, and W. Bruce Traill. Co-published simultaneously in *Journal of International Food & Agribusiness Marketing* (International Business Press, an imprint of The Haworth Press, Inc.) Vol. 10, No. 4, 1999, pp. 77-99; and: *Cross-National and Cross-Cultural Issues in Food Marketing* (ed: Erdener Kaynak) International Business Press, an imprint of The Haworth Press, Inc., 1999, pp. 77-99. Single or multiple copies of this article are available for a fee from The Haworth Document Delivery Service [1-800-342-9678, 9:00 a.m. - 5:00 p.m. (EST). E-mail address: getinfo@haworthpressinc.com].

The Haworth Document Delivery Service: 1-800-342-9678. E-mail address: getinfo@haworthpressinc.com <Website: http://www.haworthpressinc.com>]

KEYWORDS. Market segmentation, pan-European, yoghurt, means-end chains, marketing strategies

1. INTRODUCTION

Market segmentation is mainly applied to domestic markets. International market segmentation has probably not received similar attention, despite the internationalization of competition largely resulting from falling trade barriers that makes it necessary for firms to focus on international strategies. As has been noted by Traill (1997) much of this growth in international trade is intra-industry trade which relies on cross-country segments of consumers. In an increasingly competitive international environment, and with technological innovation enabling manufacturers to develop a wide product mix, it is important for these firms to be able to understand the similarities and differences in consumption patterns among consumers in their various target markets.

The purpose of this paper is two-fold. Firstly, the authors intend to stress the strategic importance of international segmentation, using the EU market as an example and the food sector as a case study. Second, a pan-European segmentation study based on an innovative measure of consumer-product relations is presented, applied to a selected food product, yoghurt. The potential strategic implications of pan-European consumer segments for food companies are also briefly discussed.

Section 2 discusses the importance of developing new approaches to market segmentation with respect to international food markets. In Section 3 the reasons for choosing the European yoghurt market for the segmentation study are discussed. Section 4 presents the development of the pan-European market segmentation exercise and discusses the results. In Section 5 the strategic implications of cross-country segments at the managerial and public policy level are discussed. Finally, Section 6 presents conclusions and some issues for future research.

2. INTERNATIONAL SEGMENTATION OF EU FOOD MARKETS

Given the heterogeneity of most markets, segmentation strategies allow for the identification of homogeneous groups of consumers likely to respond in similar ways to a particular marketing mix. For firms operating in an international environment accurate market segmentation assumes a key role given differences among countries due to cultural, socio-economic and political conditions. In a number of cases macro variables such as economic indicators, geographic location, political status and religion have been used to segment international markets to obtain "country segments" (Jain, 1990, 358-368; Baalbaki and Malhotra, 1993). The limitations of such studies are that they do not account for variation within countries and, in ignoring culture and history, create unlikely bedfellows such as Japan and Austria (e.g., Helsen et al., 1993). Their usefulness in predicting consumption is therefore limited.

The emerging Single European Market, encouraged by the elimination of trade barriers, stimulates market competition and requires firms operating in this market to base decisions on the dictates of a range of European consumers. Questions therefore arise as to whether the EU can be treated as one homogeneous market, or whether nation states maintain their own individual patterns of consumption. This leads to the question of whether pan-European segments exist, and if so how such segments can be identified and their characteristics described.

The debate on the globalization of consumer markets has produced a number of studies investigating the convergence of such consumption patterns. In the food sector, Herrmann and Roder (1995) study the convergence of food consumption in the OECD countries by analyzing the demand trend for food nutrients. Gil et al. (1995) investigate the relationship between economic development and food consumption trends in the EU, testing the convergence towards a common diet with respect to calorie intake. Both studies conclude that signs of convergence are present, although the convergence process could be a very slow one. However, convergence in consumption patterns does not mean uniformity, especially if convergence is measured on nutrient intake rather than actual product consumption. Askegaard and Madsen (1995) investigate the homogenization of food cultures within Europe by grouping regions according to respondents' attitudes towards foods and eating behavior. It seems that culture remains an important separating factor, with not only countries but also regions likely to maintain their own identities with respect to food consumption behavior.

Attitude and behaviors common to consumers across Europe mainly refer to the search for convenience, more variety in foods, better and consistent quality of food products and concern over health (Steenkamp, 1996; Uhl, 1993; Leeflang and van Raaij, 1995). Grunert et al. (1993) have created a tool to measure food-related lifestyles based on consumers' attitudes towards food, ways of shopping, cooking and eating behavior. Subsequently, Brunso et al. (1996) have used this instrument to segment food consumers in four EU countries. The study concludes that there are grounds to justify cross-country consumer segments with respect to food-related lifestyle, although consumers belonging to a particular segment would not necessarily show preference for the same type of food products.

In this paper an alternative segmentation procedure is used, based on means-end chains. The statistical methodology for market segmentation based on means-end chains was developed in the context of the EU funded AIR project "A Consumer-Led Approach to Foods in the EU: Development of Comprehensive Market-Oriented Strategies" by ter Hofstede, Steenkamp and Wedel (1997b). The main aims of the research project are to improve international market segmentation strategy in a pan-European context with respect to food products, and to identify new market opportunities for selected foods. Here, we present the segmentation results for yoghurt, which are based on a survey of about 4,000 consumers in 11 EU countries, and discuss their relevance as predictors of consumption behavior and as tools for firms wishing to target pan-European yoghurt market segments.

3. THE EUROPEAN YOGHURT MARKET

An in-depth analysis of the market was based on market intelligence literature (Euromonitor, 1996; Retail Business, 1996; Mintel, 1995; Rabobank, 1994) supported by a number of interviews with marketing professionals in manufacturing companies, retail chains and trade organizations in four EU countries.

The consumption of dairy products in the EU follows a regional pattern, although a trend in the preference towards fresh, low-fat and perceived healthy products is evident throughout. As a consequence, the consumption of skimmed milk, yoghurt and fresh cheese has increased, whereas butter consumption has decreased. The overall demand for dairy products is expected to increase moderately in the EU, but the market for yoghurt and other value-added products is likely to grow faster thanks to the possibility for differentiation and new product development (Eurostat, 1995). The yoghurt market in particular has been characterized by consistent growth throughout the 1980s in most EU countries, and represents one of the most dynamic components of the dairy sector.

The recent growth of yoghurt consumption in mature markets (e.g. France) indicates that there are still market opportunities to be identified and exploited. Another factor suggesting untapped demand opportunities is the difference in the quantities consumed across the EU countries. Yoghurt consumption in the EU averages around 10 kg per capita per year (Euromonitor, 1996) ranging from about 5 kg in Italy and Ireland to over 20 kg in the Netherlands (see Figure 1).

The EU yoghurt market as a whole is dominated by a few multinational

FIGURE 1. Annual Yoghurt Consumption in the EU, 1994 (kg per capita)

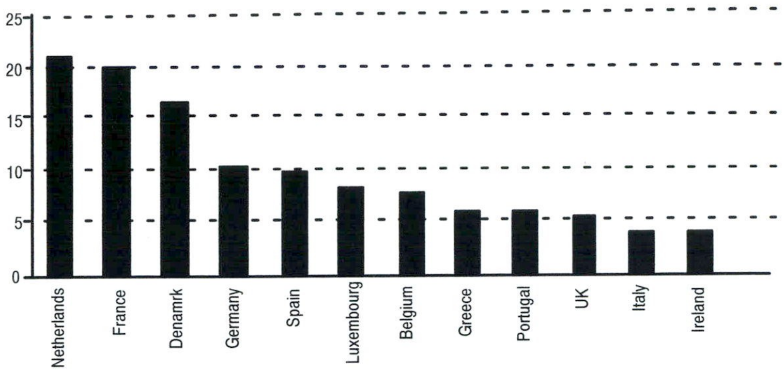

Source: Adopted from *Euromonitor, 1996.*

companies that account for about 60% of the total market and either produce yoghurt in, or export it to, a number of European countries. Medium to large companies serve either national or regional markets and their activities increasingly relate to the supply of retailers' private labels. Other small to medium companies have to take advantage of the remaining market opportunities. For these companies, the identification of regional, national or cross-national segments, which may be too small to be of interest to the large companies, could be of considerable importance. They may include niche markets, which the SMEs are well equipped, and flexible enough, to work in.

Demographic factors are a major influence on yoghurt consumption. In particular, consumption appears to be high among the younger age groups, women, households with children, and the higher strata of income and education levels. In general, consumer preference for yoghurt appears to be mainly dictated by the perceived healthiness of the product on the one hand and taste on the other, although significant differences do exist across countries. The marketing professionals interviewed unanimously attribute such differences to culture and tradition, which are considered responsible for different preferences with respect to various yoghurt characteristics (e.g., mild/sour taste, thick/thin texture, pack-size, consumption occasions), as well as consumption levels.

The yoghurt market shows a high degree of product differentiation, either by yoghurt attributes or by the information given to the consumer through advertising. The spectrum of product differentiation includes the characteristics shown in Figure 2.

The market also shows a high level of product adaptation activity, although core product innovation appears rather modest and new products

FIGURE 2. Dimensions of Yoghurt Differentiation

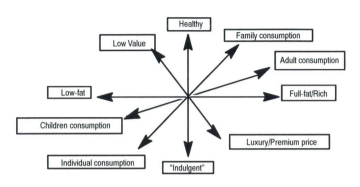

seem to result mainly from reformulation, new flavors and new packaging. Growth through new product development is mainly expected in the indulgence/luxury end of the market, but the "health" factor remains important, and the market for low-fat, probiotic and organic products[1] is expected to grow in the future.

The price of yoghurt differs significantly from country to country due to different pack sizes, retail structure, private labels' share of the market, manufacturing structure, the level of market competition, and advertising expenditure. Industry interviewees identified several main bases for competition in the market, namely price, quality, access to distribution and good relationships with retailers, efficient logistics, wide product range and adequate investments in communication.

4. SEGMENTING THE EUROPEAN YOGHURT MARKET

Due to the difficulty of establishing meaningful links between consumers' characteristics and actual behavior, recent developments in consumer research propose ways of relating consumer characteristics to their preference for product attributes. This paper describes a new approach to pan-European market segmentation by which consumer segments are identified on the basis of the Means-End Chain (MEC) approach (Gutman, 1982). The MEC approach defines product attributes as *means* by which consumers obtain desired *ends* (values) through consequences yielded by those attributes (Gutman, 1982). Means-end chains are ultimately represented by the linkages consumers indicate between product *attributes,* the *consequences* yielded by those attributes, and the *values* those consequences lead to. According to ter Hofstede et al. (1997a, p. 1760) "means-end chains can be seen as consumer-product relations that extend the notion of product benefits to the value level." The MEC approach is related to theories of consumer motivation, consumer cognitive structure and categorization processes, as it assumes that "values are centrally held cognitive elements which stimulate motivation for behavioral response. They exist . . . in a hierarchical structure in which global values are connected to generalized consumption-related values which are, in turn, similarly associated with product attributes" (Vinson et al., 1977, p. 49).

Values can be defined as centrally held beliefs and are considered to be relatively stable over time and universally accepted, and are therefore regarded as suitable for cross-cultural comparisons. The problem with such values is the difficulty in relating them to product preferences or actual choice.

The MEC approach finds a solution to the problem by linking values to consumers' perceptions of product characteristics.

The main means-end chains with respect to yoghurt were derived through in-depth interviews using the laddering technique introduced by Reynolds and Gutman (1988). Yoghurt attributes were elicited through preliminary interviews and combined with other attributes found in the literature to obtain a list of yoghurt characteristics important to consumers. Product attributes were used as the starting point in the in-depth interviews for uncovering the associations consumers make between yoghurt attributes and the consequences from using a certain type of yoghurt, and between these consequences and the values perceived as important. With this technique, consumers are continuously asked some form of the question "why is that important to you ?", which forces them from the concrete level of product attributes "up the ladder" to the more abstract level of values. One hundred in-depth interviews for yoghurt were conducted in Belgium, half of which in Wallonia and half in Flanders. Belgium was chosen because its cultural variation can represent, on a small scale, the variation in cultures within the EU.

Given the heterogeneity of individual responses in laddering interviews, the number of concepts resulting from the interviews must be compacted into a smaller number of categories. The concepts arising at the value level from the laddering interviews with respect to yoghurt were found to be consistent with the value-concepts included in the List of Values (LOV) proposed by Khale (1983). Therefore, the value items eventually included in the segmentation questionnaire were directly extracted from the LOV.

Laddering is a time-consuming and expensive method, thus it is only suitable for small scale surveys. The Association Pattern Technique (APT) was used as an alternative method to collect means-end data on the large scale required for systematic analysis. As suggested by Gutman (1982), the APT is based on the fact that means-end chains can be seen as a series of interconnected matrices through which it is possible to express Attribute-Benefit[2] and Benefit-Value associations (on the use of the APT as an instrument to measure means-end chains see ter Hofstede et al., 1998). The yoghurt attributes, benefits and values previously uncovered were included in two matrices: an Attribute-Benefit (AB) matrix and a Benefit-Value (BV) matrix, which represent the core items of the questionnaire used in the segmentation survey. The APT task for the consumers taking part in the survey consisted of indicating firstly the associations between Attributes and Benefits, and then those between Benefits and Values, by ticking the corresponding boxes in each relevant matrix.

It seems important, however, to underline that the APT simplifies the means-end approach to three-level chains, whereas the flow of speech characteristic of one to one interviews easily produces a more complex network of concepts going from product attributes to values. As it is discussed in various literature (e.g., Olson and Reynolds, 1983; Mulvey et al., 1994), a product can be defined on *concrete* attributes and abstract attributes; in turn, the consequences can be defined as *functional* or *psychosocial* and values can be either *instrumental* or *terminal*. From this viewpoint a means-end chain can be represented by a network where the levels can range from three to six or more, because also attribute-attribute, consequence-consequence and value-value associations are possible. By using the APT, the levels of the resulting means-end chains are pre-defined.

The APT matrices designed for yoghurt in Belgium were incorporated into a questionnaire and administered to samples of 100 consumers in Denmark, Greece and the UK for cross-cultural validity. The list of concepts included in the final APT matrices with respect to yoghurt is shown in Table 1.

The final questionnaire also included a wide range of background variables to capture as much of the complexity in consumer behavior, personality and attitude as possible. Consumer-specific variables include household characteristics, media consumption, general personality and attitude data (e.g., consumer ethnocentrism and environmental consciousness). Food-related variables include measures of attitude towards foods in general (e.g., quality consciousness, health consciousness, price consciousness). Yoghurt-specific variables include product knowledge and involvement, attitudes to-

TABLE 1. Yoghurt Attributes, Benefits and Values Included in the APT Matrices.

Attributes	Benefits	Values
With fruit	Good for your health	Fun and enjoyment in life
Bio-bifidus	Good quality	Self-respect
Organically produced	Good if you are on a diet	Security
Low-fat	Good taste	Excitement
Mild	Good for the digestion	Self-fulfillment
Low priced	Replaces unhealthy snacks	Being well-respected
High priced	Convenient to use	Sense of accomplishment
Packed in individual portions	Environmentally friendly	Sense of belonging
	Spend less money	Warm relationships with others
	Choice for each member of the family	

wards yoghurt, yoghurt consumption and purchasing behavior, preferences for yoghurt attributes, and benefits sought from yoghurt consumption.

The identification of the yoghurt segments is based on the probability of each respondent indicating Attribute-Benefit and Benefit-Value linkages, which depends on the consumers' perceived importance of each linkage and on their overall response tendencies, that is the propensity to express a linkage at all (ter Hofstede et al., 1997a).

Results

The segmentation exercise resulted in four cross-country clusters for yoghurt. The resulting means-end chains for each segment are represented by hierarchical value maps (HVM), where the attributes are at the bottom oft map, the benefits in the middle and the values at the top (see Figures 3 to 6).

As can be seen from the HVMs, for each of the four segments the segment-specific linkages are shown. The higher is the probability that a linkage be chosen, the thicker is the arrow between the two concepts in the map (see below). Each segment is characterized by the number and type of linkages, and by the yoghurt concepts thus indicated. On this basis it is possible to discriminate across segments and identify the elements on which a segment specific strategy can be developed. Additionally, the differences between segment-specific linkage probabilities and the aggregate linkage probabilities were calculated at the *attribute-benefit* and *benefit-value* level to identify the

FIGURE 3. Hierarchical Value Map for Segment 1

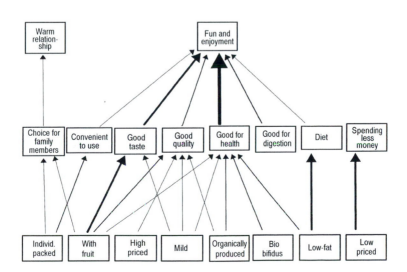

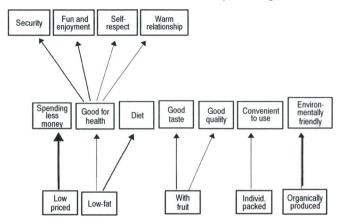

FIGURE 4. Hierarchical Value Map for Segment 2

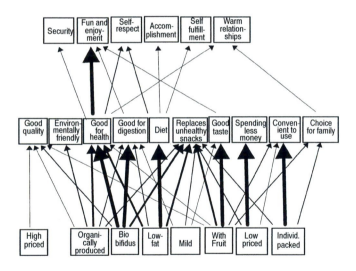

FIGURE 5. Hierarchical Value Map for Segment 3

particularly strong or weak linkages for each segment. It is beyond the scope of this paper to provide a thorough description of all four yoghurt segments, so only the main discriminating factors will be illustrated.

Common linkages are found in all four means-end chains. At the *attribute-benefit* level, the linkages common to all four segments are the associations between "With fruit' and "Good taste," "Low-fat" and "Diet," "Low priced" and "Spending less money" and between "Individually packed"

FIGURE 6. Hierarchical Value Map for Segment 4

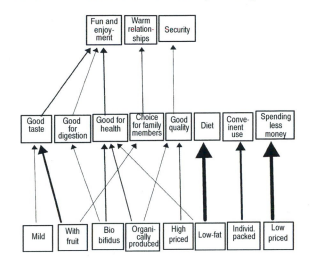

and "Convenient to use." At the *benefit-value* level, the linkage between "Good for health" and "Fun and enjoyment" is common to all segments. Given that the means-end chain conceptual model is that "values, defined . . . as desirable end-states of existence, play a dominant role in guiding choice patterns" (Gutman, 1982, p. 60) and that "values provide consequences with positive or negative valences. . . Therefore, the values-consequences linkage is one of the critical linkages in the model" (Gutman, 1982, p. 61), incomplete linkages are assumed to be unimportant as determinants of choice. Therefore, AB linkages not associated to any value and BV linkages not associated to any yoghurt attribute are disregarded when analyzing the segments.

Segment 1

Consumers in Segment 1 indicate a number of yoghurt characteristics as quality and health cues. Thus, quality and healthiness could be used as positioning concepts. The complete linkage associating fruit yoghurt with tasting good which ultimately leads to having fun and enjoying life is common to other segments, but appears to be stronger in Segment 1. "Fun and enjoyment" is the dominant value in this segment. The association low-fat yoghurt as being good for diet with having fun and enjoying life differentiates this segment from the others.

Segment 2

The overall structure of the means-end map for Segment 2 is much simpler, suggesting a lower involvement of consumers with yoghurt. Low-fat represents a health cue. In contrast to Segment 1, "Being good for health" is associated with four values by consumers in Segment 2.

Segment 3

Segment 3 shows a much more complex structure, suggesting that consumers in this segment consider yoghurt as an important food in their diet. "Organically produced," "Bio-bifidus" and "Low-fat" are important indicators of yoghurt healthiness and are associated with being good for digestion. These two benefits are in turn associated with "Fun and enjoyment." Another discriminating linkage is the association between "Low-fat" and "Diet," leading to three values.

Segment 4

The two strongest complete linkages in Segment 4 are between yoghurt with fruit and tasting good, and between bio-bifidus organically produced yoghurt with being good for health, both leading to "Fun and enjoyment." However, these linkages, if less strong, are common to other segments as well. High priced and being organically produced are indicators of good yoghurt quality, leading to security. This linkage differentiates Segment 4 from the other segments.

"Fun and enjoyment in life" is the dominant value in all four segments, and is therefore not a determinant in differentiating the segments. The number of values changes from segment to segment, as does the complexity of means-end structures, suggesting diverse consumer involvement with yoghurt. What actually discriminates between segments is the overall structure of each means-end map. Especially in those segments where few values arise, it seems legitimate to consider whether yoghurt consumption only depends on goals such as "having fun" (e.g., Segment 1). As a consequence, the question arises as to whether values actually add any insight to the motives driving consumption. Research on cross-cultural laddering conducted in Denmark, Finland, France and the UK aimed at identifying important means-end chains with respect to vegetable oils and beef shows significant country differences in the motives driving food consumption.[3] In particular, if compared to consumers in the other three countries, British consumers appear to be motivated rarely by personal values when choosing food products. British consumers' choice seems to be mainly dictated by pragmatic motives (e.g., spend less money) rather than by abstract values (Nielsen, 1998). Further research on means-end chains is needed to validate the hypothesis that such structures can actually explain the consumption of a product.

Similarly, the legitimacy of the APT and the independence of AB linkages from BV linkages should be considered. The tests conducted in this particular study justify the use of APT as an alternative to laddering, but some doubt remains whether the separation of the two linkages does not contradict the original means-end conceptual model. Further empirical evidence of the validity of APT is required.

Relating Profiles to Segment Membership

The complete segment profiles are obtained by relating consumers' segment membership to the additional background variables collected through the survey, as Table 2 illustrates.

The profile variables shown in Table 2 were assessed for each segment by means of least squares regressions. The "+" and " − " signs are the signs of the coefficients of the regressions of each profile variable on the individual segment membership probabilities, where the intercept is restricted to the mean value of the dependent variables. A positive (negative) sign[4] indicates that the attitude, behavior or status of consumers in a segment is significantly above (below) average ($p \leq 0.05$). All regressions produce quite low R^2 values, though, due to the fact that segment membership probabilities can not explain a large proportion of the variation in individual profile variables.

As to personality profiles, Segments 1 and 2 are less likely to consume foreign products than the other segments. Consumers in Segment 1 are involved with yoghurt, care about health and are quality conscious, but also are conscious about prices and likely to switch between brands. Consumers in Segment 2 show little involvement with yoghurt (consistent with the simple structure of their means-end chain) and are mainly concerned with yoghurt convenience as a diet food and as a substitute to unhealthy snacks. Segments 3 and 4 appear more innovative and involved with yoghurt. Consumers in Segment 3 seem to be mainly interested in yoghurt as a substitute for unhealthy snacks, whereas consumers in Segment 4 are more interested in yoghurt quality and healthiness. Segments 1 and 3 mainly consume yoghurt as a snack.

Consumers in Segments 1 and 2 are relatively older than consumers in Segments 3 and 4 and have a lower level of education and income. Consumers in Segment 2 live in smaller communities and prevalently purchase yoghurt in corner shops and at the market. On the contrary, consumers in Segment 4 live in larger communities and primarily buy yoghurt in hypermarkets or other large stores. Consumers in Segment 2 show the highest TV and radio consumption, whereas consumers in Segment 1 prefer newspapers and magazines. Consumers in Segment 3 mainly listen to the radio and read newspapers, whereas consumers in Segment 4 show the lowest overall media consumption.

Personality data, attitudes and product involvement are particularly valuable in the process of product positioning, promotion strategy (e.g., price

TABLE 2. Segment Profiles.

	Segment 1	Segment 2	Segment 3	Segment 4
Are consumers in this segment...?				
Quality conscious	+	−	−	+
Price conscious	+			−
Looking for change		−		+
Deal prone	+	−	+	−
Health conscious	+	−	−	
Environmentally conscious		−		+
Ethnocentric	+	+	−	−
Innovative in food consumption	−		+	
Searching for information		−		
Involved with yoghurt		−		+
Informed about yoghurt		−		+
or they have a positive attitude towards yoghurt?	+	−	+	
What benefits are important to them about eating yoghurt?				
Good if they are on a diet	−	+		
Convenient to use		+		
Replacing unhealthy snacks	−	+	+	−
Spending less money	+	−	−	−
Good for health	+	−	−	+
Good quality	+	−	−	+
Good taste	−			
When do they eat yoghurt?				
As a dessert		−		
Between meals	+	−	+	
As part of a starter		+		−
Where do they buy yoghurt more often?				
At the supermarket			+	−
At the hypermarket or superstore	+	−	−	+
In dairy produce or corner shops	−	+		
At the mini-market or convenience store		+		−
At the market		+		−
Household characteristics				
Age of main shopper	+	+	−	−
Highest level of education	−	−	+	+
Number of children	−			
Income after tax	−	−	+	+
Size of the place of residence	−			+
Media consumption				
Listen to the radio at weekdays		+	+	−
Listen to the radio at weekends		+		−
Watching TV at weekdays		+		
Watching TV at weekends		+	−	−
Watching films				+
Watching serials		+	−	−
Watching talk shows		+		−
Watching entertainment programs		+		−
Watching sports		+		−
Reading daily newspapers	+		+	−
Reading weekly magazines	+	−		
Shopping behaviour				
Frequency of food shopping	−		+	
Spending on groceries during past 7 days		−		+
Spending on yoghurt during past 7 days		−	−	+

promotion) and communication. Media consumption data are obviously useful in media planning for communication strategy, and shopping profiles help in the definition of distribution strategy. Yoghurt consumption profiles can be used in product strategy, where the characteristics of the product itself are suggested by the attributes present in the means-end maps. The study does not provide sufficient information to be used in pricing decisions, so only general guidelines can be provided at this stage on whether a segment is more or less likely to accept higher or lower prices. Apart from that, the information collected is sufficient to suggest an overall marketing mix specific to target each segment.

Geographical Location of Segments

At this point the segments may be geographically located. Table 3 presents the size of the segments in each country. Segment 4 is the largest and is especially common in the Southern European countries. Being represented by at least 22% of consumers in each country, Segment 4 is a clear example of a *pan-European* segment. Segments 1, 2 and 3 can be defined as *cross-country* clusters. Segment 1 is represented by a large proportion of German consumers, but is also significantly represented in Portugal, France and Belgium. Segment 2 is well represented in Denmark, the UK, Ireland, the Netherlands and Portugal. Segment 3 is well represented in Denmark, Germany and the UK.

5. MANAGERIAL AND PUBLIC POLICY IMPLICATIONS

The existing literature on the subject testifies that market segmentation is far from being an exact science. A whole range of approaches using different

TABLE 3. Segment Proportions by Country.

	Segment size(%)			
	Segment 1	*Segment 2*	*Segment 3*	*Segment 4*
Belgium	17.5	12.2	8.5	61.8
Denmark	2.6	47.6	27.0	22.8
Germany	45.1	3.2	26.3	25.4
UK	7.0	41.2	26.0	25.9
France	21.8	2.4	3.3	72.4
Greece	13.4	28.2	6.5	52.0
Ireland	12.1	40.6	17.9	29.5
Italy	10.2	5.9	5.1	78.8
Netherlands	14.3	31.5	17.9	36.3
Portugal	27.8	35.2	4.9	32.1
Spain	8.5	25.1	3.8	62.6
Total*	*20.9*	*17.4*	*15.8*	*46.0*

* Segment proportions are calculated as weighted averages of country-specific segment proportions

methodological tools as well as different types of consumer measures can be used to identify segments in a particular market. For this reason, it is important to determine whether means-end chains, as yet another methodological tool, add to the realism of any market segmentation study. To do that it is necessary to investigate what implications such an approach has at both a managerial and a public policy level. Figure 7 suggests how the information obtained through the identification of pan-European segments can be used by managers in a way that benefits consumers as well as the firm. While means-end chains are not specifically viewed as a tool for public policy making, Figure 7 also suggests that the information could be useful input to formulating a range of public policies.

Managerial Implications

The information contained in a segment-specific means-end chain can be used in a straightforward way to develop new product concepts, *ad hoc* product positioning concepts and a framework on which market communication can be created.

As Figure 8 shows, each level of a means-end chain provides an input for strategy development. The product attributes most featured in a particular chain are especially relevant for consumers in the segment and can be used to define the characteristics of the product designed to target that segment. At the second level of the chain, the association between product attributes and benefits can be used to define the positioning concept for the product. At the upper level of the chain, the complete attribute-benefit-value linkages can be used to develop the framework for communication strategy. One of the main benefits from the identification of pan-European or cross-country segments is the possibility for a firm to develop a standardized communication strategy which can be used to reach consumers that belong to the same segment, but live in different countries. The same is true concerning the development of standard concepts for product positioning. While a new product aimed at a cross-country segment could still need some adaptation in terms of product characteristics and price before being marketed in different countries, the means-end chain approach seems to offer an important basis for developing international communication strategy. An example of a framework for the development of market communication on the basis of means-end chain information is provided in Figure 9. The first column contains a section of the means-end chain for Segment 3. On the basis of the structure and concepts present, a rough example of guidelines to develop an advertising communication according to the MEC is given in the column on the right. This framework provides a useful starting point from which advertising agencies can develop their creative work.

Information on the means-end chain should be used alongside profile data.

FIGURE 7. Managerial and Public Policy Implications of the Segmentation Study

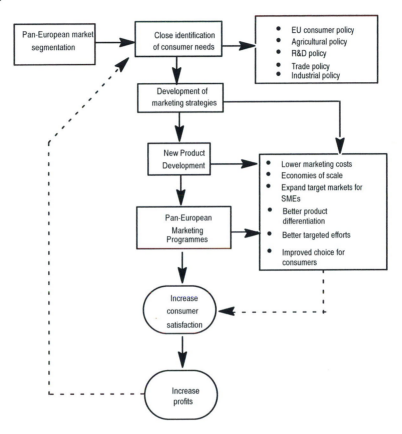

FIGURE 8. Input for Strategy Development

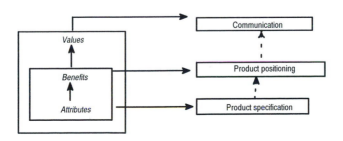

FIGURE 9. Product Communication Based on Means-End Chains

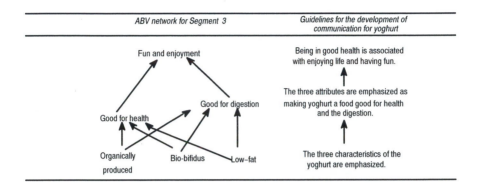

Media consumption data by segment indicates the best avenue for communication. Data on yoghurt purchase behavior indicate which type or types of retail outlet should be used to target each segment. Brand switching behavior or deal proneness in a segment indicate whether price promotion could be effective. Such strategies can be standardized at a cross-country or pan-European level to some extent, though the nature of competition and the structure of the yoghurt manufacturing and retailing sectors in the various countries will continue to influence the degree to which new marketing strategies are standardized.

Besides the managerial implications at the level of development of appropriate strategies to target specific segments, more general implications should be pointed out. First of all, the identification of pan-European segments allows for the expansion of target markets across borders. At the same time, lower marketing costs through the standardization of marketing programs may make it possible to exploit economies of scale in both production and marketing. If this is common practice for large companies and multinationals, it may not be so for smaller sized companies. Within the EU especially, given the important role that small and medium sized enterprises (SMEs) play within the food sector, cross-country consumer segments might be of interest for smaller firms that have the capability of enlarging their markets across borders. While it is doubtful that smaller SMEs would have the capacity to individually undertake such complex consumer research, they may make use of publicly funded research such as that presented in this paper (the information collected through this EU funded project is publicly available to food companies of any type and size) or collaborate with other companies to jointly fund the work through a commercial agency.

One possible drawback is represented by the costs faced by businesses wanting to develop studies based on individual consumer response, particularly at an international level. The costs of collecting primary data are likely to be higher than the costs of studies that make use of secondary data to identify market segments; for example, geoclustering approaches which use residential neighborhoods to group consumers into segments. On the other hand, the latter approaches provide less detailed consumer information and are therefore less adequate to explain specific product preferences.

Public Policy Implications

As already indicated, means-end chains are not specifically designed as a tool of public policy, but by providing more detailed information on consumer preferences with respect to product attributes, benefits and values, policies may be improved. Referring back to Figure 8, the same concepts apply to the policy maker as to the business strategist. For example, product specification and positioning is relevant to R&D policy aimed at improving industrial competitiveness through pre-competitive research of a consumer-relevant nature (e.g., on organic milk production or probiotic yoghurt cultures and their health benefits). Agricultural policy, targeting perhaps niche products for specific consumer segments (e.g., geographically denominated products), could also make use of such results. Nowadays it is also increasingly important to communicate policies and their benefits to consumers. Using the above examples, R&D policy must be "sold" on the basis of its benefits to consumers as well as industrialists, and agricultural policy on its benefits to consumers as well as farmers. The message and the communication channel are important to policy makers in most policy areas and means-end chains (along with cheaper techniques presently in vogue, such as focus groups) could provide a useful tool in policy formulation, targeting and communication.

6. CONCLUSIONS AND SUGGESTIONS FOR FUTURE RESEARCH

The questions still open concern (1) whether the results of the segmentation exercise actually identify new market opportunities, (2) whether the findings add to the knowledge of the European yoghurt market gained from the preliminary market analysis (see Section 3), and (3) to what extent the resulting cross-country segments justify the development of standardized European strategies.

The original analysis of the European yoghurt market often gave the impression of quite separate domestic markets due to both consumption reasons and structural differences. The market segmentation exercise identifies four cross-country segments, which represent common groups of consumers sharing similar attitudes to yoghurt. Nonetheless, some national markets appear to be more homogeneous than others. For example, Italy, France, Spain and Belgium present very high proportions of consumers belonging to one segment, whereas Denmark, the UK, the Netherlands, Germany and Portugal have significant proportions of consumers in at least three segments. As far as preferences and attitudes are concerned, the preliminary market analysis indicated that yoghurt's perceived healthiness and taste are the most important determinants of preference, although with some national differences. This is confirmed by the segmentation results, as yoghurt's taste and healthiness are central benefits for all the segments identified (see Figures 3 to 6), although their relative importance can differ from segment to segment. The segmentation identifies further benefits of yoghurt consumption–for example, its being good for digestion and suitable as a dietetic food–which represent further opportunities for strategic product positioning. The information collected identifies areas for better targeted product differentiation, opportunities for geographical market expansion and consequent economisation on marketing costs.

Means-end chain segments seem to provide richer information on yoghurt characteristics important to consumers in a specific segment than traditional market analysis. Means-end chain segments appear to hold important implications for product positioning and market communication, and companies willing to do so will be able to exploit economies of scale in production, but also in communication. It appears as though pan-European marketing programs can be mainly justified for market communication, and to some extent for new product development. Structural market differences, such as the level of market competition, structure of the manufacturing and retailing sectors, and consequent price differences represent constraints to the development of completely standardized marketing programs.

One of the limitations of the present study can be ascribed to the novelty of the approach used. Given that this is a first application of means-end chains as the criterion to segment European consumers with respect to food products, formal validation is needed. In this respect, further research could investigate the role that personal values actually play in motivating food product choice. The same approach could be applied to different food products and the results compared. A second research issue concerns the use of the Association Pattern Technique (APT) to collect means-end chain information. As a new methodological tool, APT needs some further validation.

Ongoing research on the same data concerns the application of more traditional techniques to identify pan-European segments on the basis of yoghurt attribute and benefit preferences alone and test the effectiveness of alternative approaches to segmentation. Furthermore, marketing strategies for each of the yoghurt segments identified are being developed and validated on a sample of consumers (independent from the sample used in the segmentation survey) in three EU countries. The validation will investigate whether consumers' perceptions and preferences for hypothetical new yoghurts and their associated marketing strategies fit the segmentation results.

NOTES

1. Probiotic yoghurts contain additional live bacteria, other than L. bulgaricus and Streptococcus thermophilous, believed to be beneficial to the human organism. Organic refers to a completely natural method of production which does not use any artificial additives.

2. Consequences can either be desired or undesired. Means-end chains elicited within the present project with respect to yoghurt only include positive consequences; in other words, benefits.

3. AIR Project "The development of models for understanding and predicting consumer food choice."

4. The signs of the regression coefficients are shown because the different scales in which the variables are expressed makes it difficult to compare the magnitudes.

REFERENCES

Antonides, G. and van Raaij, W.F. (1998). *Consumer Behavior. A European Perspective.* John Wiley & Sons (UK).

Askegaard, S., & Madsen, T.K. (1995). Homogeneity and Heterogeneousness in European Food Cultures: An Exploratory Analysis. In Bergadaà, M. (Ed), *Marketing Today and for the 21st Century (pp. 25-48).* 24th EMAC Conference, Paris, May 16-19.

Baalbaki, I.B., & Malhotra, N.K. (1993). Marketing Management Bases for International Market Segmentation: An Alternate Look at the Standardization/Customization Debate. *International Marketing Review,* 10 (1), 19-44.

Brunso, K., Grunert, K.G., & Bredhal, L. (1996). *An Analysis of National and Cross-National Consumer Segments Using the Food-Related Lifestyle Instrument in Denmark, France, Germany and Great Britain.* MAPP Working Paper no.35, Aarhus, Denmark.

Dairy Products and Eggs (1996). *Euromonitor: The European Compendium of Marketing Information,* 73-84.

Engel J.F., Blackwell R.D. and Miniard P.W. (1995). *Consumer Behavior.* The Dryden Press.

EC Dairy Facts & Figures (1994). Milk Marketing Board, United Kingdom.

European Yoghurt Markets (1995). London: Frost & Sullivan.

Gil, J.M., Gracia, A., & Perez y Perez, L. (1995). Food Consumption and Economic Development in the European Union. *European Review of Agricultural Economics,* 22, 385-399.

Grunert, K.G., Brunso, K., & Bisp, S. (1993). *Food-Related Life Style: Development of a Cross-Culturally Valid Instrument for Market Surveillance.* MAPP Working Paper no. 12, Aarhus, Denmark.

Gutman, J. (1982). A Means-End Chain Model Based on Consumer Categorization Processes. *Journal of Marketing,* 46 (2), 60-72.

Gutman, J., & Reynolds, T.J. (1986). Coordinating Assessment to strategy Development: An Advertising Assessment Paradigm Based on the MECCAS Model. In Olson, J.C., & Sentis, K. (Eds), *Advertising and Consumer Psychology* (pp. 242-258), Vol. 3. New York: Praeger.

Halliburton, C., & Hunerberg, R. (1993). Pan-European Marketing–Myth or Reality? In Halliburton, C., & Hunerberg, R. (Eds), *European Marketing. Readings and Cases* (pp. 26-44). Addison-Wesley.

Hassan, S.S., & Katsanitis, L.P. (1994). Global Market Segmentation Strategies and Trends. In Hassan, S.S., & Kaynak, E. (Eds), *Globalization of Consumer Markets. Structures and Strategies* (pp. 47-62). New York: International Business Press.

Helsen, K., Jedidi, K., & DeSarbo, W.S. (1993). A New Approach to Country Segmentation Utilizing Multinational Diffusion Patterns. *Journal of Marketing,* 57 (4), 60-71.

Herrmann, R., & Roder, C. (1995). Does Food Consumption Converge Internationally? Measurement, Empirical tests and Determinants. *European Review of Agricultural Economics,* 22, 400-414.

Jain, S.C. (1989). Standardization of International Marketing Strategy: Some Research Hypotheses. *Journal of Marketing,* 53 (1), 70-79.

Jain, S.C. (1990). *International Marketing Management* (Ch. 11). Boston: PWS-Kent.

Kahle, L.R. (1986). The Nine Nations of North America and the Value Basis of Geographic Segmentation. *Journal of Marketing,* 50, 37-47.

Kale, S.H., & Sudharshan, D. (1987). A Strategic Approach to International Segmentation. *International Marketing Review,* Summer, 60-70.

Kamakura, W.A., & Mazzon, J.A. (1991). Value Segmentation: A Model for the Measurement of Values and Value Systems. *Journal of Consumer Research,* 18, 208-218.

Kamakura, W.A., Novak, T.P., Steenkamp, J-B.E.M., & Verhallen, T.M.M. (1993). Identifying Pan-European Value Segments with a Clusterwise Rank-Logit Model. *Recherche et Applications en Marketing,* 8, 29-55.

Leeflang, P.S.H., & van Raaij, W.F. (1995). The Changing Consumer in the European Union: A *"Meta-Analysis." International Journal of Research in Marketing,* 12, 373-387.

Lilien, G.L., & Kotler, P. (1983). *Marketing Decision Making: A Model Building Approach* (Ch. 11). Harper & Row Inc.

Mulvey, M.S., Olson, J.C., Celsi, R.L., & Walker, B.A. (1994). Exploring the Relationships Between Means-End Knowledge and Involvement. *Advances in Consumer Research,* Vol. 21, 51-57.

Nielsen, N.A. (1998). Personal Communication.

Olson, J.C., & Reynolds, T.J. (1983). Understanding Consumers' Cognitive Structures: Implications for Advertising Strategy. In Percy L., & Woodside, A.G. (Eds), *Advertising and Consumer Psychology (pp. 77-90).* Lexington Books.

Panorama of EU Industry 95/96 (1995). EUROSTAT, 13, 27-36.

Reynolds, T.J., & Gutman, J. (1988). Laddering Theory, Method, Analysis, and Interpretation. *Journal of Advertising Research,* February-March, 11-31.

Shocker, A.D., & Srinivasan, V. (1979). Multiattribute Approaches for Product Concept Evaluation and Generation: A Critical Review. *Journal of Marketing Research,* XVI (May), 159-180.

Steenkamp, J-B.E.M. (1996). Dynamics in Consumer Behavior with Respect to Agricultural and Food Products. In Wierenga, B. et al. (Eds), *Agricultural Marketing and Consumer Behavior in a Changing World.* 47th Seminar of the EAAE, Wageningen, Netherlands, March 13-15, 15-38.

ter Hofstede, F., Steenkamp, J-B.E.M., & Wedel, M. (1997a). Segmenting International Markets on the Basis of Consumer-Product Relations. In Arnott D. et al. (Eds), *Proceedings of the 26th EMAC Conference* (pp. 1759-1764). Warwick Business School, May 20-23.

ter Hofstede, F., Steenkamp, J-B.E.M., & Wedel M. (1997b). *International Market Segmentation Based on Consumer-Product Relations.* Working Paper, Wageningen University (submitted for publication).

ter Hofstede, F., Audenaert, A., Steenkamp, J-B.E.M., & Wedel M. (1998). An Investigation into the Association Pattern technique as a Quantitative Approach to Measuring Means-end Chains. *International Journal of Research in Marketing,* 15 (1), 37-50.

Traill, W.B. (1997). Globalization of the Food Industries. *European Review of Agricultural Economics,* 24 (3-4), 390-410.

Uhl, J.N. (1993). Comparisons of Food Marketing systems in the EU and the USA: The Market Convergence Hypothesis. In Meulenberg M. (Ed), *Food and Agribusiness Marketing in Europe* (23-36), NY: The Haworth Press, Inc., 23-36.

Vinson, D.E., Scott, J.E. & Lamont, L.M. (1977). The Role of Personal Values in Marketing and Consumer Behavior. *Journal of Marketing,* 2, 44-50.

Walker, B.A. & Olson, J.C. (1991). Means-end Chains: Connecting Products with Self. *Journal of Business Research,* 22, 111-118.

Wierenga, B. (1983). Model and Measurement Methodology for the Analysis of Consumer Choice of Food Products. *Journal of Food Quality,* 6, 119-137.

The World Dairy Industry. Developments and Strategy (1994). Rabobank, The Netherlands.

Yavas, U., Verhage, B.J., & Green, R.T. (1992). Global Consumer Segmentation Versus Local Market Orientation: Empirical Findings. *Management International Review,* 32, 265-273.

Yoghurt (1996). Retail Business (no. 457), United Kingdom.

Yoghurts and Chilled Pot Desserts (1995). Mintel, United Kingdom.

Index